Using Information to Develop a Culture of Customer Centricity

Using Information to Develop a Culture of Customer Centricity

Customer Centricity, Analytics, and Information Utilization

David Loshin

Abie Reifer

ELSEVIER

AMSTERDAM • BOSTON • HEIDELBERG • LONDON
NEW YORK • OXFORD • PARIS • SAN DIEGO
SAN FRANCISCO • SINGAPORE • SYDNEY • TOKYO

Morgan Kaufmann is an imprint of Elsevier

Morgan Kaufmann is an imprint of Elsevier
225 Wyman Street, Waltham, MA, 02451, USA

Notices
Knowledge and best practice in this field are constantly changing. As new research and experience broaden our understanding, changes in research methods or professional practices, may become necessary.

Practitioners and researchers must always rely on their own experience and knowledge in evaluating and using any information or methods described herein. In using such information or methods they should be mindful of their own safety and the safety of others, including parties for whom they have a professional responsibility.

To the fullest extent of the law, neither the Publisher nor the authors, contributors, or editors, assume any liability for any injury and/or damage to persons or property as a matter of products liability,negligence or otherwise, or from any use or operation of any methods, products, instructions, or ideas contained in the material herein.

Library of Congress Cataloging-in-Publication Data
A catalog record for this book is available from the Library of Congress

British Library Cataloguing-in-Publication Data
A catalogue record for this book is available from the British Library.

ISBN: 978-0-12-410543-0

For information on all MK publications
visit our website at www.mkp.com

This book has been manufactured using Print On Demand technology. Each copy is produced to order and is limited to black ink. The online version of this book will show color figures where appropriate.

CONTENTS

PREFACE

INTRODUCTION

In the middle of 2012, I was approached to assemble a concise book on analytics. I saw this as an interesting challenge, since I did not want to just add another book discussing algorithms and systems that could be dumped on top of a growing pile of authoritative texts. My preference, I suggested to the editor, was to assemble a book to bridge the use of analytical applications with a business perspective that would explain not **how** to perform one analysis or another, but rather **why** an organization could derive value from such an initiative.

I selected customer centricity as the core focus of the book and reached out to my colleague Abie Reifer to work with me on it. While his training and career has somewhat mirrored my own in terms of knowledge of computer science, his intimate knowledge of a number of customer-facing industries complements my own experience on the technical side. Both of these choices have turned out to be good ones—as we have worked together on this book, we have solidified our approach to marshaling our clients through the process of envisioning, scoping, and planning for a strategy and roadmap for customer centricity.

THE CHALLENGE OF CUSTOMER CENTRICITY

What does "customer centricity" mean? I am sure that countless hours have been allocated to attempting to reach some clear definition, but instead we hope to convey more of a "description" than a definition: the ability to augment every customer interaction to provide the perception of increased value exchange for both the company and the customer. Yet this poses numerous questions, such as:

- Who is the customer?
- What is meant by value?
- How is value exchanged?
- How do you assess the future value of a customer relationship?

- How does that future value inform the decisions that are being made in the present?
- How can an organization transition from being function-focused to being customer-focused?

Our goal is not really to answer these questions; rather, our objectives include clarifying what the intent is of asking these kinds of questions and guiding the processes for effectively scoping and then answering the questions in a way that leads to increased profitability, reduced risk, and overall, an enhanced customer experience.

WHAT THIS BOOK IS

The goal of this book is to provide a firm grounding in laying out a strategy for customer centricity. It is meant to provide an overview of what customer centricity is and why it can add value, and how to properly plan to consider the need, set expectations, align the right people in the organization, and map out a strategy.

On the other hand, this book is not meant as a "how-to" for development of customer-centric algorithms or applications. Rather, our intent is to provide an overview within each chapter that addresses some pertinent aspect of the process of adopting customer centricity:

- Chapter 1—What is Customer Centricity: We consider a description of a strategy for customer centricity and explore the evolution of the approaches as a way of driving corporate value.
- Chapter 2—The Value of Customer Centricity, in which we discuss a practical perspective on the use of customer information as part of a customer centricity program, considers the facets of value that can demonstrate the utility of customer centricity, as well the facets of value that can be improved as a result of understanding your customers.
- Chapter 3—Who is a Customer, where we explore the degree to which clarifying the concept of customer becomes a critical task to precede data collection, analytics, process improvements, and change management. Precision in terminology can influence decision-making, so it is valuable to explore the concept of customer and how those considerations impact organizational customer centricity.
- Chapter 4—Customer Lifetime and Value Analytics, where we explore some of the issues and questions about assessing the future value of a relationship with a customer, and the use of data, thoughtfulness, analytics, and insight to drive a cohesive customer centricity model.

- Chapter 5—Connectivity and Spheres of Influence, where we look at the ways that individuals within the customer and prospect communities can sway the thought processes and consequently the decisions of others, especially in the ways that any customer's experience (positive or negative) may reverberate across that customer's various social networks.
- Chapter 6—Customer Touch Points and the Exchange of Value, where we discuss customer "touch points," or the method by which customer interactions occur, the types of interactions, the categorization of the "value" that is exchanged between the two parties, and then consider what information about the customer is needed for the analyses and guidance that can be used to augment those interactions.
- Chapter 7—Organizing Data for Customer Centricity, in which we look at the data requirements for building and delivering the customer profiles and then examine different approaches to accessing, integrating, organizing, and managing customer data.
- Chapter 8—Customer Profiling, where we look at the concepts of segmentation and classification and understand the types of data characteristics that provide input to assembling the different customer personas used for analysis as a way to augment customer interactions with a customer-centric flavor.
- Chapter 9—Customer Data Analytics, in which we discuss the different technical methods and algorithms used for analyzing customer data, creating customer profiles, and classification and segmentation.
- Chapter 10—Making Customer Centricity Pervasive in the Company: In this chapter, we look at the directive for cultivating the right culture for customer centricity within the company, change management, and the need for senior management commitment in both word and deed. Lastly, we review the steps discussed in the book as a starting point for developing the customer centricity strategy.

WHY YOU SHOULD BE READING THIS BOOK

You have probably picked up this book for one or more of these very good reasons:

- You are a senior manager seeking to take advantage of your organization's information to create or add to corporate value by increasing revenue, decreasing costs, improving productivity, mitigating risks, or improving the customer experience.

- You are the Chief Information Officer or Chief Data Officer of an organization who desires to make the best use of the enterprise information asset.
- You are a manager who has been asked to develop a customer centricity program.
- You are a manager who has been asked to take over a floundering customer-facing application or program.
- You are a manager who has been asked to take over a successful customer-facing application or program.
- You are a senior business executive who wants to explore the value that customer centricity can add to your organization.
- You are a business staff member who desires more insight into the way that your organization does business with its customers.
- You are a database or software engineer who has been appointed a technical manager for a customer centricity program.
- You are a software engineer who aspires to be the manager of a customer centricity program.
- You are a business analyst who has been asked to join a customer centricity application team.
- You are just interested in customer centricity.

OUR APPROACH TO KNOWLEDGE TRANSFER

As I have mentioned in the prefaces to my previous books ("Business Intelligence—The Savvy Manager's Guide, Second Edition," "Master Data Management," and "The Practitioner's Guide to Data Quality Improvement"), I remain devoted to helping organizations strategically improve their capabilities in gaining the best advantage from what might be called "information utility." My prior experiences in failed data management activities drove me to quit my last "real job" (as I like to say) and start my own consulting practice to prove that there are better ways to organize and plan information-oriented program.

My company, Knowledge Integrity, Inc. (www.knowledge-integrity. com) was developed to help organizations form successful high-performance computing, business intelligence, analytics, information quality, data governance, and master data management programs. As a way of distinguishing my effort from other consulting companies,

I also instituted a few important corporate rules about the way we would do business:

1. Our mission was to develop and popularize methods for enterprise data management and utility. As opposed to the craze for patenting technology, methods, and processes, we would openly publish our ideas so as to benefit anyone willing to invest the time and energy to internalize the ideas we were promoting.
2. We would encourage clients to adopt our methods within their success patterns. It is a challenge (and perhaps in a way, insulting) to walk into an organization and tell people who have done their jobs successfully that they need to drop what they are doing and change every aspect of the way they work. We believe that every organization has its own methods for success, and our job is to craft a way to integrate performance-based information quality management into the existing organizational success structure.
3. We would not establish ourselves as permanent fixtures. We believe that information management is a core competency that should be managed within the organization, and our goal for each engagement is to establish the fundamental aspects of the program, transfer technology to internal resources, and then be on our way. I often say that if we do our job right, we work ourselves out of a contract.
4. We are not "selling a product," we are engaged to solve customer problems. We are less concerned about rigid compliance to a trademarked methodology than we are about making sure that the customer's core issues are resolved, and if that means adapting our methods to the organization's, that is the most appropriate way to get things done. I also like to say that we are successful when the client comes up with our ideas.
5. Effective communication is the key to change management. Articulating how good information management techniques enhance organizational effectiveness and performance is the first step in engaging business clients and ensuring their support and sponsorship. We would invest part of every engagement in establishing a strong business case accompanied by collateral information that can be socialized within and across the enterprise.

With these rules in mind, our first effort was to consolidate our ideas for semantic, rule-oriented data quality management in a book,

"Enterprise Knowledge Management—The Data Quality Approach," which was published in 2001 by Morgan Kaufmann. I have been told by a number of readers that the book is critical in their development of a data quality management program, and the new technical ideas proposed for rule-based data quality monitoring have, in the intervening years, been integrated into all of the major data quality vendor product suites.

Since 1999, we have developed a graduate-level course on data quality for New York University, multiple day courses for The Data Warehousing Institute (www.tdwi.org), presented numerous sessions at conferences and chapter meetings for DAMA (the Data Management Association), course and online content for DATAVERSITY (www.dataversity.net), provided columns for Robert Seiner's Data Administration Newsletter (www.tdan.com), monthly columns for DM Review (www.dmreview.com), a downloadable course on data quality from Better Management (www.bettermanagement.com), and hosting an expert channel and monthly newsletter at the Business Intelligence Network (www.b-eye-network.com) and TechTarget (www.TechTarget.com).

We are frequently asked by vendors across the spectrum to provide analysis and thought leadership in many areas of data management. We have consulted in the public sector for both federal, state, and other global government agencies. We have guided data management projects in a number of industries, including government, financial services, health care, manufacturing, energy services, insurance, and social services, among others.

Since we started the company, the awareness of the value of information management has been revealed to be one of the most important topics that senior management faces. In practices that have emerged involving the exploitation of enterprise data, such as Enterprise Resource Planning (ERP), Supply Chain Management (SCM), and Customer Relationship Management (CRM), there is a need for a consolidated view of high-quality data representing critical views of business information. Increased regulatory oversight, increased need for information exchange, business performance management, and the value of service-oriented architecture are driving a greater focus on performance-oriented management of enterprise data with respect to utility: accessibility, consistency, currency, freshness, and usability of a common information asset.

CONTACT US

While our intention is that this book will provide a guide to concepts for a customer-centric strategy, there are situations where some expert advice helps get the ball rolling. The practices and approaches described in this book are abstracted from numerous real client engagements, and our broad experience may be able to jump-start your mission for deploying a customer centricity program. In the spirit of openness, we am always happy to answer questions, provide some additional details, and hear feedback about the approaches that we have put in this book and that Knowledge Integrity has employed successfully with our clients since 1999.

We are always looking for opportunities to help organizations establish the value proposition, develop the blueprint, roadmaps, and program plan, and help in implementing the business intelligence and information utilization strategy, and would welcome any opportunities to share ideas and seek out ways we can help your organization. We really want to hear from you.

David can be reached via his email address, loshin@knowledge-integrity.com, through Knowledge Integrity's company website, www.knowledge-integrity.com, or via www.davidloshin.info.

ACKNOWLEDGMENTS

DAVID'S ACKNOWLEDGMENTS

My wonderful wife Jill deserves the most credit for her perseverance and encouragement in completing this book. I also must thank my children, Kira, Jonah, Brianna, Gabriella, and Emma for their help as well.

ABIE'S ACKNOWLEDGMENTS

I would like to thank my loving wife Rikki and my children Miri, Danielle, and Rachel for their patience and continued support on (nearly) all of the projects that I embark upon.

GENERAL ACKNOWLEDGMENTS

What is presented in this book is a culmination of years of experience in projects and programs associated with best practices in employing data management tools, techniques, processes, and working with people. A number of people were key contributors to the development of this book, and we take this opportunity to thank them for their support.

Critical parts of this book were inspired by as material presented through David's expert channel at www.b-eye-network.com, adapted from presentation material at conferences hosted by Wilshire Conferences, DATAVERSITY, DebTech International, The Data Warehousing Institute (www.tdwi.org), and vendor-hosted sources including The Data Roundtable (http://blogs.sas.com/content/datamanagement/), and my blog entries for Melissa Data (http://blog.melissadata.com/mt-search.cgi?blog_id=2&tag=David%20Loshin).

CHAPTER 1

What Is Customer Centricity?

INTRODUCTION

Although over recent years the volume of customer interactions has greatly accelerated, a conceptual social contract still connects companies to their customers in the desire to provide quality products and impeccable customer service that binds both together throughout the customer's lifetime. In reaction to the accelerated speed and frequency, and consequently the "depersonalization" of the customer interaction, there have been numerous industry initiatives over the past few years that have promoted concepts centering on business strategies and approaches to maintain acceptable, if not exceptionable, levels of customer satisfaction.

These concepts are often broadly bundled using the term "customer centricity." Customer centricity incorporates ideas, approaches, strategies, and tactics which have evolved over time in alignment with different industries' customer-oriented initiatives. All of these initiatives share one key notion: focusing operations around the company's customers as a way to increase customer loyalty, reduce churn and attrition, and increase revenues, resulting in the delivery of superior product and service to the customer community.

While customer centricity is an evolving set of practices, this introduction will set the stage for understanding how customer-facing initiatives center on improved treatment of the customer. This provides a perspective that highlights how, despite certain differences in approach, most of the concepts are directed at improving the customer experience. In turn, this book will look at the relationship between improved customer experience and the creation and maintenance of corporate value.

Next, we examine the fundamental concept of the customer—who is a customer and how many ways that customer can be engaged. Forming a relationship with the customer goes beyond the simple sales transaction, and in some cases that relationship not only occupies a significant time period but may also survive across different parts of an individual's life or even span multiple generations within a family

Figure 1.1 Hello Mert? Is that you? How's every little thing?

or a community. We look at how customer-centric strategies and processes are to be leveraged at the different touch points to maximize value and consider how customer data can be organized and then used for customer profiling and customer analytics. We then discuss the critical dependence on pervasive institutionalization of customer centricity directly into company processes and procedures. To optimize for the creation of corporate value, you can assess your business in relation to the strategies presented, determine how customer relationships are intertwined with the success of your business, and then consider the approaches that are best suited for your business.

THE EVOLUTION OF CUSTOMER CENTRICITY

Before the age of electronic commerce, one might presume that customer care was relatively easy to provide. Because businesses were less complex and comparatively small when compared to current standards, establishing and retaining relationships with customers were relatively straightforward.

For example, consider the old-time switchboard operator shown in Figure 1.1,[1] who knew every person with a telephone connected

[1]Downloaded on September 22, 2013 from http://www.loc.gov/pictures/item/owi2001021042/PP/.

through her switchboard. The operator's direct and personal knowledge enhanced the experience of the caller.

In fact, in many smaller environments, the owners or the workers at retail product or service businesses had direct, long-term relationships with the customers—knowing many facts about them, such as their children's names, their birth and anniversary dates, and potentially even more intimate details. Knowledge of these details added to the process and therefore achievability of customer centricity—engaging the customer on a personal level helped in building relationships with each of the customers and providing them with personalized care. Even larger businesses had sales managers who built relationships with their clients. Managers knew their customers well, regularly interacted with them and were able to ensure the company understood their clients' needs. This was all part of providing customers with a personalized and human touch. It may not have been sophisticated in its reliance on technology, but it worked.

As businesses grew due to a significant increase in the number and variety of clients, they often had a need to increase staff in order to scale up their customer support operations. But the very nature of supporting an expanding customer base meant that these managers would need to share the burden of building customer relationships with new staff. The growth of the sales staff had consequences—increased employee turnover, reduced personal interactions with customers, etc., all led to less personal interactions with the customers. The result is that the business relationship with the customer suffered.

More succinctly, as businesses grow, they often commoditize what was once the distinctive characteristics of their relationships with and treatment of their customers. In turn, as companies grew and competition increased it became more difficult to provide the same level of care. Customer loyalty waned and retaining customers became more difficult. Companies touted their priority on the customer using customer-oriented marketing slogans like "the customer is number 1." And over the past few years, there have been numerous initiatives, revolving around a variety of customer focused strategies. The number of acronyms and buzzwords on the subject has often created confusion.

In other words, those same companies pushing the concept of the customer often lacked the strategies and tools to provide adequate personalized care. As a result their marketing campaigns rang hollow. Even as many businesses have tried to focus on their customers, as businesses grow, their ability to provide the "personal touch" that previously may have been a differentiator has become more difficult to maintain.

CUSTOMER EXPERIENCE AS A CORPORATE DRIVER OF VALUE

The idea that customer experiences can be managed within the context of a relationship and subsequently automated is not new. Customer Relationship Management (CRM) systems have been in production for a number of years and are intended to comprise a set of strategies intended to help organizations provide scalable customer service for a growing customer community. More specifically, CRM approaches are intended to incorporate systems that would capture customer information regarding the customer. This information can be used to help organizations develop and improve their internal processes so that managers could more easily exchange customers and maintain a relationship with the client.

In reality, though, CRM was also intended to help identify efficiencies in the organization by providing replicable customer support and service functions that scale efficiently, thereby reducing the average cost of customer service on a per-customer basis. In other words, although the initiative was intended to center on the customer, the real focus was to enable the scalability of the services provided to customers.

Curiously, businesses that had historically offered differentiated and personalized customer care began to realize that the CRM strategies they implemented were causing their business to lose what was once a personal touch cherished by their clientele and what likely had differentiated the business from others. In essence, commoditizing their treatment of customers ultimately disenfranchised those very customers that had earlier helped them establish their business.

The recognition that this commoditization of care which diminished the customer relationship has led to considering different strategies designed to engage the customer by focusing on the overall experience in conjunction with the relationship. This approach is less concerned with operational efficiency and instead is intended to let the staff members be more proactive and anticipatory of the customer's needs and expectations. Concentrating on enhancing the customer's overall experience helps to provide the customer with the perception of personalized treatment.

For example, a company may be able to make product suggestions to the different customers based on their earlier purchases.

This is commonly predicted by reviewing the combination of products and/or services a customer has made then comparing those purchases to ones made by others and suggesting products by others having similar interests. Being able to make suggestions of products that compliment the ones already purchased by the customer is an example of a predictive customer-centric approach. Customers often appreciate being informed of related products or services, since that provides them with a sense of individualized and differentiated service.

INCREASING CORPORATE VALUE BY INTEGRATING CUSTOMER VALUE ANALYTICS INTO THE ENTERPRISE

A customer-centric approach helps to increase corporate and customer values. Many companies seek opportunities for upselling and cross-selling additional products or services to their customers. This approach is beneficial to both the companies through the generation of increased revenue at presumably lowered cost, as well as the customer who can be provided with bundled complementary items also at a presumably lowered cost. By using improved analysis and predictive methods, the company's presentation of recommended offers will be welcomed by the customer as long as the practice is managed well and does not seem to be intrusive or obnoxious.

Customer-centric strategies can vary greatly. Some incorporate significant levels of sophistication such as seeking to increase customer loyalty over time by providing cumulative positive experiences. Retaining customers through loyalty building through progressive positive and personalized interactions will lead to elongating the customer's lifetime and increasing their long-term satisfaction.

Some of the key distinctions that enable companies to migrate from their operation-based CRM program to a fully customer-centric strategy is their willingness to learn about their customers, analyze how that knowledge can influence better business processes and decisions, and integrate those results into their customer interactions, or as they are also called customer touch points. These often result in new or enhanced product or service offerings or other interaction improvements such as customer care service center operations and procedures. As the customer analyses lead to more valuable impacts, the ability to employ and exploit more sophisticated analyses enables businesses to incrementally tweak their offerings and continually improve the way they handle their customers.

CUSTOMER DATA VISIBILITY

Many companies operate multiple lines of business, resulting from organic growth or as a result of serial mergers and acquisitions. From an operational standpoint, in companies that operate in this fashion, there is little motivation for the individual lines of business to share information. As an example, companies in the telecommunications industry will provide a broad array of services, including wireline telephony, wireless telephony, internet service, as well as television, home automation, and home security services. Yet the marketing, sales, fulfillment, and customer service associated with each of these services are likely to be provided through different divisions, if not entirely separate business entities.

Nonetheless, companies that sell complementary products and services want to leverage an existing relationship and expand it so that the company–customer bond is strengthened through increased commitment on both sides. That requires a critical adaptation and use of shared data about the customer drawn from all available resources.

Customer data visibility is a customer centricity tactic that enables the business to have increased knowledge about any specific customer by collecting data from across different business applications, identifying those records that are associated with a specific entity, and then integrating those records together. This allows the business to have a holistic view and understanding of the customer, which can facilitate the types of analyses that can enable better-informed processes for marketing, for cross/upselling products and services, for improved customer service, and ultimately improved customer satisfaction and retention.

CUSTOMER INTERACTION MANAGEMENT

Achieving very personalized and individualized care is the next stage that some companies, even large ones, are looking to achieve. Customer interaction management methods begin with analyzing a broad set of interactions associated with sets of customers compared with interactions of individual customers and the types of decisions that resulted from those interactions. Understanding how different types of interactions can influence decision making helps companies build customer loyalty by using the knowledge derived from that unified customer view. This approach can help companies to develop models reflecting customer intimacy materialized through offers of personalized and targeted products and services to their customers.

An example is the supermarket loyalty card program. Customers who regularly shop at the same supermarket and use their loyalty card may not realize that every purchase they make helps the grocer incrementally build a detailed profile about the customer's purchasing patterns. These patterns can be incorporated in delivery of targeted coupons that are produced at checkout, but are increasingly being used for proactive marketing campaigns (such as coupons delivered through the mail or via email), or even real-time delivery to mobile devices while the customer roams the store.

SUMMARY: CUSTOMER VALUE IS CORPORATE VALUE

There is one key theme that we hope to carry throughout this book: improved customer centricity leads to increased value to both the company and the customer. Ultimately, the objective of a customer-centric strategy is to deliver the optimal service to each customer on a personalized level. Different types of customers may warrant different types of service, and we hope to share some ideas about:

• how to segment customers into differentiated categories,
• how classification schemes can be used to modulate your interactions with your customers,
• how these interactions can be informed through customer data visibility and customer data analytics, and
• how business processes can be adapted to take best advantage of a customer-centric strategy.

The definition of customer centricity may still be evolving, but for our practical purposes it represents a set of strategies that places the customer at the center of an organization's operations. These strategies and methods are intended to help companies and organizations better understand who their customers are, what they want, and how they can best benefit symbiotically.

CHAPTER 2

The Value of Customer Centricity

CUSTOMER CENTRICITY AND THE CONCEPT OF VALUE

Before launching into greater detail on the methods and mechanics of managing customer centricity, it might be wise to ask a straightforward question: What is the value of a customer-centric strategy? The typical response to this type of question involves some general statements about having a "360-degree view of the customer," or "crossselling and upselling," yet these relatively obtuse statements still beg the question, since having visibility into a broad view of any customer's profile does not imply what that profile means to the business or even if the company has put processes in place to take advantage of that customer profile.

More accurately, the question can be rephrased to yield a practical perspective on the use of customer information as part of a customer centricity program: What are the facets of value that can demonstrate the utility of customer centricity? Even more directly, what are the facets of value that can be improved as a result of understanding your customers? At a very high level, we can propose five different fundamental facets of value, as is depicted in Figure 2.1:

1. Revenue
2. Costs
3. Risk
4. Productivity
5. Customer experience

The relevance of these facets of value can be considered in different contexts. For example, a company's CEO might be interested in a rolled-up report of corporate profitability that balances and blends measured metrics for corporate revenue and corporate expenses. A manager of one of the company's divisions might look to increase the productivity of the staff members that work for that division. On the other hand, a customer will seek to derive the optimal value from the investment in a company's product or service.

Figure 2.1 Facets of value.

Ultimately, a strategy for customer centricity should be directly connected to an optimal combination of these different facets of value. This optimal combination must integrate increased value from both the company's and the customer's perspectives. The value of customer centricity can be demonstrated when enhancing the customers' experiences helps increase revenues, limit costs, reduce risk, and improve productivity.

BUSINESS EXPECTATIONS AND PERFORMANCE METRICS

While the objective of a customer centricity program is to create and improve value, it is often difficult to quantify that value for three related reasons. First, in most cases there are only fuzzy approximations of the anticipated benefits that can be achieved. This is especially true when the motivations for the program solely revolve around expectations for increased value without considering how the customer profile information is to be used to influence the creation of value. Second, because the expectations are not well defined, neither are performance metrics, and no measurements of the current state are performed prior to the beginning of the program. Improvement cannot be determined when there is no baseline with which to compare. Third, no continuing measurements are performed to track improvements in value.

A pragmatic approach to monitoring the success of a customer centricity program begins with the determination of the facets of value that you anticipate improving and then assessing the relationship between improved customer information and reaching your company's goals. This can be broken up into four key steps:

1. Identify specific business expectations for creation or improvement of value.
2. Characterize the performance metrics and measurement methods for each of those business expectations.
3. For each measure of performance, describe the ways that improving the customer's experience can lead to increased value.
4. For each expectation of improved value, determine the business processes that need to be adjusted or changed to achieve the desired effects.

We can summarize the process using the image in Figure 2.2.

In the following sections, we examine the different facets of value in greater detail. In addition, we provide a number of examples of applying these steps to model how to refine business objectives for customer centricity, how to select performance metrics, and importantly, consider ways that the business processes must evolve to achieve the desired results. Each of these examples will identify the *business expectation*, the *performance metrics*, and the *link to the customer experience* and discuss some examples of *business processes* to be introduced or adjusted.

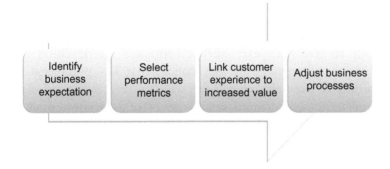

Figure 2.2 Linking performance metrics to customer centricity.

REVENUE GENERATION

This facet of value focuses on improving activities that increase profitability through revenue generation. Some example activities include:

- Increase same-customer sales, involving increasing the item count or financial volume of sales to existing customers.
- Improve customer retention, centering on growing the relationship with each existing customer to elongate the duration of the relationship, and its qualitative aspects.
- New customer acquisition, focusing on identifying new geographies, new customer segments, or new product markets.
- New product creation, which researches ways to leverage corporate intellectual property in innovative ways or to acquire or repackage original equipment manufacturer (OEM) new products.
- Product bundling, in which collections of products can be bundled in ways that increase profitability while satisfying customer expectations and needs.
- Increase marketing of profitable products, especially when the effectiveness of increased marketing investment can be directly tied to increased sales.
- Revise product pricing strategies, which evaluates how product prices effect purchasing decisions, whether prices need to be adjusted, and how pricing changes on one product impact the end-to-end supply, production, and sales of other products.
- Increase revenues from alternate investments, such as productization of information products, leveraging real property for rental revenue, portfolio investments, banking decisions, etc.

As an example, let us focus on increasing same-customer sales. The business expectation might involve identifying the "best customers" and increasing that cohort's average number of purchased products from four to five per year. The performance metric could then be defined as the percentage of that cohort that has purchased five or more products over the year. One way to link improved customer experience to these increased sales is to offer a promotion such as a special discount or an additional premium item to the best customers who increase their annual sales.

There could be a number of new processes or existing business processes that would need to be adjusted as a result, such as:

- Introduce customer profiling to identify the "best customers."
- Adjust marketing plan to promote the offer to those best customers.
- Train sales team to reach out to the members of the cohort and communicate the promotional offer.
- Alert inbound call center staff that when a "best customer" calls for support to notify that customer of the opportunity to take advantage of the promotional offer.

DECREASING COSTS

This facet of value focuses on improving activities that increase profitability by reducing expenses. Some examples include:

- Improving supply chain processes, which looks at the different costs of acquiring raw materials and bringing them into the physical plant to see if they can be acquired at a lower cost, using less expensive means of transport, or lowering the costs of product delivery. The lowered costs of a more efficient supply chain create savings that can be passed to the customer.
- Increasing the speed of fulfillment, which seeks to speed the delivery of ordered product to the customers while maintaining the same costs or even reducing delivery costs.
- Improving targeted marketing, with the goal of reducing the amount of money spent on marketing campaigns by directing crafted campaigns at specific market segments. This leads to better targeted marketing messages that may resonate with specific customer profile types on a more personalized level.
- Lowering the costs of customer support, with the objective of reducing the aggregate costs for providing customer support, including call center staff, resources, warranty costs for addressing customer dissatisfaction. Efficiencies at the call center may enable faster response times for inbound calls as well as more streamlined customer service.
- Managing customer retention costs by reducing the monetary costs of premium offers to retain customers.

As an example, let us focus on improving supply chain processes. The business expectation might be lowering the cost of shipment of raw materials. The performance metric could be defined as the average cost of shipment by material type by finished product, with the objective of a 1% reduction in the annual shipping costs. One way to link improved customer experience to lowered shipping costs is that if the company can reduce the cost of goods sold, the cost savings can be passed through to the customer by lowering the cost of the final product.

There could be a number of new processes or existing business processes that would need to be adjusted as a result, such as:

- Vendor analysis focusing on shipping vendors to determine those that can provide reliable service at the lowest cost.
- Redesign products to use less material, which would improve the utilization of raw materials across a larger number of products.
- Identify strategic manufacturers of raw materials located close to your company's factories to reduce the shipment distances.
- Transition to a just-in-time manufacturing process to reduce the need to maintain large stocks of raw materials, thereby reducing the warehousing costs.

REDUCING RISK

This facet of value focuses on improving activities that reduce operational, financial, compliance, or other types of risk. Some examples include:

- Credit analytics that can be used to narrow the potential risks of customer payment default, lengthy time for collection of receivables, or even restricting sales to customers who pose a credit risk.
- More efficient operational reporting, which not only provides better insight into the cumulative performance of various activities across the organization, it also enables better decision-making.
- Compliance management that focuses on identifying behaviors or activities that are misaligned with regulations, which if not addressed can lead to fines or expose the organization to legal action.

IMPROVING PRODUCTIVITY

This facet of value focuses on improving activities that optimize the use of existing resources. Some examples include:

- Optimizing employee performance, perhaps through incentives for good customer service.
- Increasing manufacturing throughput by ensuring machinery is maintained properly and monitoring the environment for stresses that can affect performance.
- Increasing manufacturing volume by maintaining productive use of existing machines and materials and better asset utilization.

As an example, let us focus on credit analytics. The business expectation might be that more accurate analysis of customer credit worthiness would not only be more precise in identifying credit risks but would also determine a greater number of customers that are expected to pay their obligations in full in a timely manner. Therefore, one performance metric could be defined as the average time-to-payment (i.e., the elapsed time between issuing an invoice and the time that customer payments are received) for the customers that have had their credit limit increased. One way to link improved customer experience to more accurate credit analytics is that there is a segment of customers whose purchase limits would be increased, allowing greater flexibility in making purchase decisions.

There could be a number of new processes or existing business processes that would need to be adjusted as a result, such as:

- Reviewing and improving the processes for customer credit analysis.
- Ensuring that all sales activities that validate credit worthiness are migrated to using the improved analytics process.
- Creating a marketing campaign targeted at those customers whose credit lines might be increased.

BALANCING CORPORATE AND CUSTOMER VALUE: ENHANCING THE CUSTOMER EXPERIENCE

This final facet of value focuses on improving activities that enhance the full life cycle of the customer experience. Including customer experience as the final component in the collection of the different facets of value completes a virtuous cycle—improving processes for increasing revenues, decreasing costs, etc. will eventually lead to an improvement in the customer experience. At the same time, enhancing the customer experience will lead to increased satisfaction, elongated customer lifetimes, and result into increased profitability. Some examples include:

- Making customer service more efficient, either by resolving issues faster or ensuring the warranty associated with dissatisfaction.
- Increasing the number and quality of customer recommendations that can be leveraged for goodwill purposes in market awareness and publicity.
- Increasing participation in loyalty programs that strengthen the customer relationship.
- Providing VIP service to high-value customers.
- Identifying underserved geographic areas and opening new branches to serve customers in those areas.

In the long run, the creation of value for the customer is symbiotic with the creation of value for the company. And as we suggest within the remainder of this book, it will become clear that there are some key activities that a company can perform that can increase the customer's lifetime value and in turn, increase corporate value.

CHAPTER 3

Who Is a Customer?

WHO IS A CUSTOMER?

The common use of the term "customer" hides a somewhat complex ambiguity. It is one of those words whose presumed meaning is so well-understood that it is infrequent that any organization actually has documented a definition. Yet in any initiative focused on customer centricity, clarifying the concept of customer becomes a critical task to precede data collection, analytics, process improvements, and change management. Precision in terminology can influence decision-making, so it is valuable to explore the concept of customer and how those considerations impact organizational customer centricity.

In retrospect, over the past 20 years, the industry analysts, popular technical press, and technology vendors promoting customer relationship management often use phrases such as "360-degree view of the customer" or "single source of truth about the customer" to suggest that it is possible to have a single business application that can address the conglomeration of all business process requirements necessary to support the introduction of customer-centric policies and processes. These types of phrases resonate with people in any business function whose processes have a customer touch point, such as sales, marketing, support, or customer service. And while from each business function's standpoint, the defined characteristics of a customer may be clear, across functions there may be subtle differences in what is understood to be meant by the term "customer."

These subtleties may be irrelevant from a purely operational standpoint, but may have impacts for analytical models that consolidate collections of customer data convened from across the different business function sources. Semantic or structural differences that do not pose any material conflict typically won't introduce any inconsistencies. But there are times that differences in meanings may lead to nonsensical aggregations. For example, the sales department might define a *customer* as "the entity that has paid for the product," while the support department defines the *customer* as "the individual with the right to request support."

DEFINING THE CONCEPT OF CUSTOMER—AN EXAMPLE

Not only might these be different entities, they might not even be related. Consider a hotel with a fitness center. The hotel management might pay for an elliptical machine that is placed within the fitness center that is used by the guests, managed by staff members who are employed by the fitness center, with the equipment maintained by an external service provider. In this scenario, there are at least six potential parties (a term that we can use as a place holder for an entity with whom the elliptical machine company interacts) that could be defined as the customer:

1. The **hotel** paid for the elliptical machine.
2. The **fitness center** "owns" the elliptical machine.
3. The **finance manager at the hotel** authorized the actual payment for the elliptical machine.
4. The **fitness center staff members** oversee the use of the elliptical machine.
5. The **hotel guests** use (and may have questions about using) the elliptical machine.
6. The **external maintenance company** services the elliptical machine.

More details about the presumed customer relationship are provided in Table 3.1, and it sheds some light on the touch points the elliptical machine manufacturer might want to manage. However, if the manufacturer wanted to create an analytical environment used to track all customer interactions, different departments might have independent databases with information about one or more of these entities. And because the perception of a customer differs across these different departments, if all these customer data sets were merged together into a data warehouse or an analytical application, the aggregated count of customers will be inconsistent from any business function perspective.

So how do you answer the question of "who is a customer?" in a way that enables consistency in reporting and analysis? And more importantly: how can you solidify the definitions so that analytical results can be used to enhance the customer experience?

Table 3.1 Characterizing the Customer Roles		
Party	**Authority**	**Touch Points**
Hotel	Owner of budget and completed payment for the product	Marketing Sales Fulfillment
Fitness center	Houses the product Responsible for continued operations of the product	Fulfillment Maintenance Retention
Finance manager	Individual authorizing payment	Marketing Sales Fulfillment Upsell/cross-sell Retention
Fitness center staff	Oversight Maintenance Management of products	Fulfillment Maintenance
Hotel guest	Uses the product	Maintenance Sales
Eternal maintenance company	Maintains the product	Maintenance Retention

HOLISTIC ENGAGEMENT IDENTIFIES THE CUSTOMER

Basically, getting a single definition for "customer" will be a perennial problem in data usability for customer centricity. The variations in explicit or implicit definitions can lead to inconsistencies in reports, "customer analytics," and resulting customer profiles that are supposed to inform any of processes for customer interaction.

To continue our example in which there is a collection of potential customers for a company that manufactures elliptical machines sold to hotel fitness centers, recognize that each interaction and touch point provides a means of branding and marketing the product and the company. Consider one particular use case in which one of the elliptical machines stops working correctly:

- A hotel guest experiencing the failure will report it to one of the fitness center staff members.
- The fitness center staff member will contact the external maintenance company to evaluate and fix the problem.
- The maintenance person comes in, checks out the machine, and determines that a part needs to be replaced, and that the broken part should be covered under the machine's warranty.

In this scenario, each potential customer's experience will influence his/her perception of the quality of the product and perception of the manufacturer in slightly different ways. Of course, at this point, the desired outcome of the process is to have the machine fixed as quickly as possible so that it can be put back into productive use at the fitness center for the benefit of the hotel guests. However, which customer will be expected to initiate the support process? Is it the hotel guest who experiences the failure? The fitness center staff member? Or the finance manager acting as the guardian of the hotel's investment?

From the perspective of the elliptical machine's manufacturer, rapid customer support may be a differentiating factor for driving product sales, and to promote the perception of rapid customer service, the manufacturer might not care who calls, as long as there is traceability associated with the process ensuring that the broken machine is indeed under warranty. As far as the manufacturer is concerned, any of those parties is the "customer," and awareness of the various relationships among those parties is valuable in ensuring the fastest response.

Examining specific use cases such as this example demonstrates the folly of attempting to come up with a single definition of customer. In essence, any individual playing any role as part of a business process can be considered to act in a role of "customer." In other words, the operational definition of "customer" can include any party with whom the organization interacts, and the operational scenario characterizes the attributes necessary for providing customer service (i.e., supporting the customer touch point). Using that definition, we can suggest that customer centricity involves more than just knowing which individuals or organizations qualify as customers; rather, it means understanding the ecosystem that emerges around the life cycle events of the customer relationship.

REFLECTIONS: CUSTOMERS AND CUSTOMER CENTRICITY

The fitness equipment example may seem somewhat contrived, but it is crafted to prove a point: any company must understand a complex set of customer relationships to ensure the provision of a desired level of customer support. In turn, there is a challenge of discerning exactly who the customers are, and through this examination one might challenge the desire to have a single definition of customer because *there is no single definition of customer.* Different individuals or organizations play different aspects of the "customer" role at different times and that attempting to homogenize the concept of customer might be counterproductive.

In essence, any individual or organization with which your business has a touch point plays one aspect of the role of customer. Any interaction with a party is an opportunity for strengthening the corporate relationship with that party, polishing the corporate brand, and establishing goodwill within the market. Treat every interaction as a *customer-centric* interaction. To be customer-centric means developing processes, training staff members, and instituting measures for enhancing the experience of any party with whom there is a customer relationship.

ENTITY VERSUS ROLE

Different parties play different types of customer roles within different use cases and processes. At the same time, there may be different processes that engage the same parties acting in different roles. The trick lies in enhancing your processes to ensure that all party interactions (even ones that are not specifically "customer-oriented") are customer-centric. That suggests that there is value in segregating the concept of "customer" from the party *playing the role* of the customer, implying the need to determine who a party is as well as the role that party plays in the different facets of each business context.

Again, the fitness center example helps to demonstrate: the hotel finance manager authorizing the payment for the elliptical machine plays the role of customer along a financial facet. The technician from the external maintenance company plays the role of customer along the service contract facet. The hotel guest who might call the company to get instructions on how to best use the machine might be playing the role of customer along a user support facet. And so on among the entire breadth of customer roles and facets.

Instead of trying to create a single view of a customer, recognize that there are multiple views that drive the creation of value in different ways. This realization will help in showing how managing the aspects and facets of customer information can help in developing a strategy for customer centricity.

SUMMARY: DRIVING CUSTOMER CENTRICITY

The perceived definition of a customer can help drive a corporate strategy for customer centricity, especially when recognizing the many different facets of the customer role that can be played by individuals at different times in different scenarios. That realization also allows us to consider some high-level suggestions for how a customer centricity strategy can create value in the organization:

- Consider every interaction with any entity (individual or organization) in which there is an exchange of value as a customer interaction.
- Treat every business process touch point as an opportunity for exchanging value.
- Presume that the data collected from every business process touch point has potential for improving your organization's methods of customer profiling.
- In each business process, examine how customer touch point data can contribute to creating value, either by leading to increased revenues, decreased costs, reduced risks, improved productivity, or through enhanced customer experiences.

Internalizing these concepts should lead to the desired outcomes of business value improvement. In particular, these ideas are fundamentally dependent on data, information, and information services that enhance the creation of actionable knowledge driving profitable customer centricity interactions and decisions.

CHAPTER 4

Customer Lifetime and Value Analytics

THE VALUE OF THE CUSTOMER

Much of the conventional wisdom and guidance for an organization's relationship with its customers is largely linked to a general recommendation that all customers are of equal value and importance. We are bombarded with aphorisms about customer relationships and interactions: "the customer is always right," "the customer is king," or "it's about the customer, always." The common themes seem to convey the idea that the goal of any business is to consistently and continuously ensure that every single customer is completely satisfied. And to some extent, there is some wisdom in suggesting that customers be treated well, since a business cannot survive without customers.

In reality, though, not every customer is the same, nor is each customer equally valued. A quick web search about the distribution of profitability at banks yielded some (unscientific) results that in general the Pareto principle (aka the "80/20" rule) generally held: 20% of the customer base accounts for 80% of the profit. In one case study, the top 16% of the customer base accounted for 105% of the profit and that the bottom 28% of the customer base actually accounted for −22% or an effective loss.[1] One can interpret this factoid to draw two interesting conclusions. First, approximately one-sixth of the customer base accounted for all of the bank's profit; and second, more than one out of every five customers accounted for a loss to the bank.

This relative inequity of profitability can be seen as being somewhat troubling. At the worst, it suggests that a significant corporate effort is expended on serving low-profitable or unprofitable customers, and that certainly raises a bunch of questions about customer relationships, customer engagement, and ultimately, the relationship between customer value and customer centricity. In this chapter, we explore some of these issues and questions in greater detail, as well as the

---

[1]See Hughes, "How Banks Use Profitability Analysis" http://www.dbmarketing.com/articles/Art195.htm.

corresponding ramifications. These considerations lend some weight to the use of data, thoughtfulness, analytics, and insight to drive a cohesive customer centricity model.

DEFINING CUSTOMER VALUE

What is the value of a customer? Clearly, different types of customers have different kinds of value; and the bank case study shows different types of customers account for different levels of profitability, and consequently, value. In addition, different customers have different values over both the lifetime of the company as well as the lifetime of the customer. Attempting to quantify the value of a customer is somewhat complex, especially when organizations struggle to even define what a customer is. Fortunately, there are some strategies for analyzing customer characteristics and behaviors in relation to key dimensions of value that help in evolving a model for customer value:

- **Customer categorization:** It is a process of organizing the customer community in terms of specific groups. In our bank case study, there is an implicit stratification of customers that includes specific levels like "best customers," "good customers," and "unprofitable customers." These are not arbitrary categories; rather they are defined with respect to some set of performance measures. What are ways to stratify or organize the different types of customers, and how are those levels defined? Are they keyed to revenue? Costs associated with customer support? Risk of customer attrition? Sometimes the first step in understanding ways to interact with your customers is to look at how they can be organized in relation to the value drivers for your business.
- **Differentiation:** Presuming that there are discrete categories for customers, how do you classify each customer within those categories? This process blends the definition of customer categories with weighted measurement thresholds that can be used to distinguish customers at different levels. What are the business demographic characteristics that are common among your "best customers?" Examples of business demographics might include number of products purchased, monetary value of subscriptions, or the length of the business relationship.
- **Classification:** As opposed to what we referred to as differentiation, which focused purely on the business value criteria for assigning a

customer's category, one might instead seek to determine what are the qualitative demographic characteristics that are common among customers within the same category, such as annual income, whether they own their own home, or educational attainment, to name a few. A combination of differentiation and classification helps in developing predictive models about the future of a customer relationship.

These three processes together can be used to assess the customer community and to provide the basis for a customer value analysis.

ADDITIONAL ASPECTS OF CUSTOMER VALUE

The preceding activities shed light on some quantitative aspects of developing customer value models. In addition, there are some additional quantitative as well as qualitative aspects of managing a relationship with a customer.

One example is the cost of doing business with the customer. Many companies track the level of effort expended in customer acquisition, but do not continue to follow through in tracking the ongoing maintenance costs of the relationship. The answer to these questions factor into assessing the value of a customer:

- What is the relative cost of operations associated with customer relationship management?
- What are the average costs for customer acquisition, retention, as well as ongoing service and maintenance among all customers?
- Can these costs be estimated or calculated on a customer-by-customer basis?

These can be factored with qualitative perceptions of the investments in engagement. In other words, what is the proper level of engagement and interaction with a customer? And at what point does the level of engagement overwhelm the value of customer retention? There is a good example of setting limits on customer engagement using a story involving Southwest Airlines former CEO Herb Kelleher's response to a perennially complaining customer. This customer was responsible for a never-ending series of letters complaining about various aspects of the Southwest Airlines business model (such as the absence of first class, not assigning seats, and casual uniforms). At one point, this customer's latest rant had been escalated to the top level of the company. Herb's reaction was to immediately draw the line between customer satisfaction and retention: he wrote back: "We'll miss you."

All of these factor into a different take on customer centricity that goes beyond the conventional expectation of the always-right customer. Instead, a model for customer centricity considers the value of the customer over the duration of the customer's relationship and enables continuous refinement of the level of engagement so as to maximize "profitability" while minimizing costs and risks. And customer value analytics will prove to be a key variable in this refinement.

EVALUATING THE VALUE OF A CUSTOMER

There are different kinds of customers who provide different kinds of value at different times during the lifetime of the customer relationship. But from an objective perspective, it is valuable to develop criteria for customer valuation that are relevant within the corporate business context. These criteria can provide quantifiable measures for characterizing customer types, enable the development of customer analytics models, and help in crafting a set of customer engagement strategies that maximize the different aspects of profitability.

In a perfect model, this could be characterized as an optimization problem by enumerating a collection of variables whose positive values we would seek to maximize or whose negative values we'd seek to minimize. We can attempt to work out this enumeration from the perspective of the most desirable optimized outcome by looking at the key dimensions of customer value and profitability. This would specify different variables to be applied to each customer, or potentially to a collection of customers, including:

- Tangible aspects such as increased revenue and decreased costs.
- Material, yet somewhat fuzzy aspects such as minimizing corporate risk.
- Practical aspects such as minimizing effort of engagement or elongating the duration of the customer relationship.
- Somewhat intangible beneficial aspects such as increased goodwill and word-of-mouth positive publicity.

Another way of saying this is that the value of a customer is a function of variables such as the examples given in Table 4.1.

The general wisdom is to seek to tweak your corporate business processes for engaging the customer so as to optimize across the full palette of these value variables. Of course, attempting to only concentrate on one or a few of these aspects may impact maximizing the overall cumulative benefit.

For example, increasing the duration of the customer relationship (i.e., increasing the "customer lifetime") may be beneficial if the customer type is one that has a predictable revenue stream across the full duration of that time horizon. But if the cost of elongating the relationship increases the level of effort and costs associated with retention (i.e., increased "retention costs"), the anticipated benefit of the revenue stream may be offset by the increased costs. As another example, decreasing the investment in maintaining a customer may result in lowered overall costs, but may increase the probability of attrition, thereby reducing (or really eliminating) the predictability of the future revenue stream.

Table 4.1 Sample Variables for Customer Valuation		
Variable	**Measure**	**Description**
Revenue stream	Revenue	The net present value of the customer's revenue stream over various time horizons
Customer lifetime	Time	The duration of the customer relationship
Maintenance cost	Cost	The costs necessary to ensure the realization of the customer's future revenue stream
Risk cost	Cost	The quantified cost of risk attributed to the customer
Acquisition cost	Cost	The costs and the level of effort associated with acquiring a new customer
Maintenance cost	Cost	The costs and the level of effort associated with maintaining the customer
Retention cost	Cost	The costs and the level of effort associated with retention
Endorsement value	Revenue	A valuation of the contribution to the revenue streams resulting from the customer's endorsement across the customer's sphere of influence
Model refinement	Revenue	A valuation of the contribution to the revenue streams resulting from the customer's contributions to customer profile models

DEVELOPING A CUSTOMER VALUATION MODEL

From a practical perspective, the customer valuation model should incorporate any variable that contributes to some measurable aspect of corporate value (as discussed in Chapter 2). Some of those given in Table 4.1 seem obvious, such as the net present value of the customer's future revenue stream. On the other hand, some have correlations that are more complex to envision, such as the revenue value of improving or enhancing the customer profile model. It is worth allocating a brainstorming session to identify those variables that can possibly contribute to corporate value and populate a table like the one provided here by taking these steps:

1. Begin with an enumeration of the high-level dimensions of value.
2. Suggest variables associated with customer engagement and touch points that potentially contribute to any of those value dimensions.
3. Specify a measure of value for each of the variables.

Once that table is populated, the next step is to consider factors for weighting the measures as they contribute to the calculation of customer value. For example, if there are costs relating to customer risks, the analysts executing this refinement task would seek to ascertain which customer characteristics are relevant in identifying the key customer risks and then assessing the costs that relate to those customer risks. Some examples include investigating the relationship between the customer's credit score or the number of times the customer has a missed or late payment and the customer's overall propensity to pay on time. These identified customer characteristics coupled with the measure calculation become a part of the valuation model.

This highlights the fact that it would be a challenge to presume that a customer valuation model can be created in the absence of any history of the results of the various customer relationships and experiences. The implication is that the developed model is going to rely on analysis of customer engagement histories involving transactions and interactions at any touch point, as well as relationships between customers and products/services and between customers and other individuals. On the other hand, it also suggests that there are some key variables that contribute more significantly to the valuation than others. This implies that you can suggest a baseline model whose variables and weightings can be refined over time.

USING THE CUSTOMER VALUATION MODEL FOR CUSTOMER CENTRICITY

A customer lifetime valuation model not only provides a means of quantifying the value of the relationship with the customer, but also enables a number of ways of implementing customer centricity, both at the different engagement points along the customer engagement life cycle and at touch points within specific business processes. Operationally, this means embedding decision processes within business processes that are driven by the integration of customer profiling and customer lifetime value models. The objective is to positively influence customer behavior in ways whose outcomes are optimized across the collection of value metrics.

Here is a simple example: leveraging offers to increase airline loyalty, revenue, and customer experience. Frequent travelers may opt to allocate their airline travel "spend" across multiple carriers. At the same time, airlines offer an effective "future rebate" in the form of a "restricted currency"—airline frequent flyer miles. These frequent flyer miles are units of value that are allocated by the flight carrier to the traveler as their future rebate. These frequent flyer miles can be accumulated and exchanged for free travel, as well as premier statuses that provide specific benefits such as greater flexibility in booking frequent flyer trips, premier-level customer service, more comfortable seating, or upgrades to higher level of travel accommodations.

A specific airline may analyze their customer profiles to assess the airline's "wallet share," or the percentage of the individual's total travel spend that has been allocated to the airline. This type of analysis requires the modeling of the different customer flyer categories (such as "vacation traveler," "intermittent business traveler," all the way to "very frequent business traveler," for example), followed by developing methods or ways of determining which individuals fall into the named categories. Third, the collection of customers must be classified according to those differentiation rules into the defined categories.

This categorization and classification can then be used to identify those customers that are likely to be traveling a lot but are not using the airline as much as potentially possible. This is the determination of the airline's wallet share. The determination that there is an opportunity to capture a greater share of wallet creates a scenario for influencing customer behavior to decide to purchase from that airline instead of any other alternative. Theoretically, influencing purchase decisions has cumulative impacts to customer lifetime value:

- Improved loyalty benefits improve the customer experience.
- Improved customer experience strengthens the customer relationship.
- A strong customer relationship leads to increased purchases.
- Increased purchases continue to contribute to increased loyalty benefits for the customer.
- Increased loyalty leads to an elongated customer lifetime.

In other words, triggering an improvement in the customer's loyalty benefits leads to improved customer experience, increased revenues, increased wallet share, and longer lifetime relationships. To that end, when it becomes apparent that a target customer is a candidate for this type of influence, the airline might trigger the cycle by offering incentives for increasing the rate or volume of accumulating frequent flyer miles that ratchet the traveler into a premier status level.

CONSIDERATIONS: INFLUENCING CUSTOMER BEHAVIOR

Customer-centric relationship management processes can blend information from customer profiles with the lifetime value model to influence behaviors in a number of ways:

- **Migration into premier status levels:** We can generalize the example above to any scenario in which loyalty benefits are used as leverage for extending the customer relationship. The decision point is influenced by offers that ease the process of increased benefits. Aside from loyalty programs, other examples include various tiered special "member discounts" provided to shopping club members willing to pay for increased membership levels or ratcheting up a level when using an affinity credit card.
- **Pumping the customer's relationship network:** Providing incentives to a customer to encourage recommending your company's products or services to his/her friends.
- **VIP service:** Using the customer's lifetime value and profile to assign level of effort applied to customer touch point activities. For example, best customers have minimal call center wait times, while undesirable customers are pushed further back on the wait queue.

- **"Leveling-up" in profile:** Identifying "good" customers who have the potential to be turned into "great" customers and providing incentives for the behaviors that would ratchet the customer into a more profitable segment from a lifetime value perspective.
- **Proactive retention management:** Identify scenarios in which providing incentives for continuous reengagement of good customers as a way of elongating the relationship, as well as reducing the benefits provided to undesirable customer to encourage their attrition.

Each of these opportunities for influencing customer behavior must be weighed in terms of the overall improvement in all relevant aspects of value over the anticipated customer lifetime. It means recognizing that sometimes what appears to be optimal for one performance measure in the short term may not necessarily be the best decision for other performance measures for the long term. For example, lowering the price of one product to increase overall number of products sold may reduce the risk of attrition, lead to a reduction in customer credit risk, or even increase product profitability by clearing out the inventory more quickly. Providing a full refund for a returned item may reduce revenue as well as incur an immediate cost of processing, but the goodwill generated may increase positive word-of-mouth, thereby increasing the network value of the customer.

In all of these cases, decisions that may seem to decrease immediate value may lead to increased lifetime values for a broad range of customers. Managing the decision processes with this perspective should increase overall profitability over the long term.

CHAPTER 5

Connectivity and Spheres of Influence

INTRODUCTION

An important aspect of customer centricity considers the ways that individuals within the customer and prospect communities can sway the thought processes and consequently the decisions of others. One conventional example is the "customer reference" or recommendation in which one customer's positive experience is used as a testimonial to encourage others to make a purchase. Alternatively, customers with negative experiences may broadcast their dissatisfaction with a vendor to their friends and neighbors and convince them not to become engaged with that vendor.

This implies that any customer's experience (positive or negative) may reverberate across that customer's various social networks. This suggests that the customer value model can be augmented to incorporate knowledge about the customer's sphere of influence—the degree to which a customer's experiences impact those of others within his/her network of connections.

CUSTOMER CONNECTIVITY CONCEPTS

Interestingly, the intersection of customer centricity and social connectivity is a common theme. For instance, when you consider the development of strategies for integrating customer centricity into the breadth of business applications in different business functions, a frequent focus is on social media analytics. The concept typically encompasses a variety of types of analyses including text analysis and sentiment assessments that can help in organizing the content within the different contexts of selected social media channels. However, there is a more fundamental type of social network analysis with a much longer pedigree that seeks to identify connections among different actors within an environment, and is particularly suited to analyzing *customer connectivity*.

Customer connectivity embodies the idea that the relationships exist between customers, among sets of customers, as well as among customers and other entities such as locations and products, and those connections and relationships can provide advantage in the creation of value. And while in the past a person's "social network" consisted of a real collection of people with whom the person had an established relationship, today's electronic means of social connectivity provides a greater base of information that can be used to support the assessment of the value of an individual's network.

The best way to begin is to look at the types of roles that exist within a network. There are archetypical roles relating to connectivity that exist within any community; one very accessible treatment of these roles is provided by Malcolm Gladwell in his book "The Tipping Point."

Gladwell shares three terms related to social network connectivity:

1. *Connectors* are those individuals who know many others and are comfortable and able to introduce one to another.
2. *Mavens* are individuals with special knowledge about a particular topic and are willing to share that knowledge.
3. *Salesmen* are individuals with skills at both persuasion and negotiation.

The right environment and combination of individuals with these roles can trigger an "epidemic" or increase in uptake of any type of behavior, such as the purchase of a particular smartphone, the decision to get a tattoo, or choosing a pay-TV provider.

In other words, it is valuable to understand the roles individuals play within a community along with the relationships among the individuals within that community. This provides an opportunity to analyze customer connectivity, seek out interesting relationships and pattern, and essentially model how social network structures and patterns influence customer behaviors. Once those patterns and structures are identified, you can strategically take advantage of the way customers are influenced within the network to create competitive advantage and increase corporate value.

MODELING THE TYPES OF CUSTOMER CONNECTIONS

Your community of customers, like any other community, consists of a collection of individual parties, which can also be referred to as "actors" that are related to one another. These relationships can be modeled using the graph abstraction, in which every actor is represented as a node, and every connection between two actors is represented as a link or an edge between two nodes.

For example, if one actor is friends with another actor, that would be represented as two nodes with one edge between them, as is shown in Figure 5.1.

However, not all relationships are necessarily reciprocal. For example, actor A may be the father of actor B, while actor B is the daughter of actor A. These relationships would have to be modeled slightly differently to show the direction of the relationship, as shown in Figure 5.2, with a directed edge between them. This also allows you to refine the nature of the relationships between actors within a community.

This abstraction can be used to represent any relationship among a set of actors, such as households, schoolmates, people who work in the same industry, and so on. Not every relationship is between two customers either. One customer might have purchased one of your company's products—one node represents the customer, the other represents the product, and the edge between them would indicate that the customer purchased that product. Alternatively, the customer might have bought the product from a particular sales channel, which in its own right could become another represented entity. In this way, we can build up a connected network representing the ways that the different actors are related. The network model becomes the basis for

Figure 5.1 A simple undirected graph.

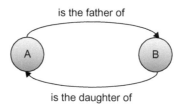

Figure 5.2 A directed graph embeds relationship information.

a number of different analyses for understanding and taking advantage of ways some customers can influence the behaviors of others.

THE CUSTOMER NETWORK: SPHERES OF INFLUENCE

The graph approach provides an effective abstraction for representing relationships among a community of actors and entities, and therefore, customer connectivity (as reflected in the many different types of actors, entities, and relationships) can be modeled within a connectivity graph.

Any defined conceptual roles can be mapped to critical positions within that social network, and those mappings embody the different types of customer connections. For example, let's consider what the topology of Gladwell's different types of connections in a customer connectivity graph would look like:

- The *connector* is an individual who knows many others and is willing to make introductions among that community. In the connectivity graph, this customer will have both incoming and outgoing connections to many others, and there will be connections between pairs of customers that he/she is connected to.
- The *maven* is an individual with special knowledge who is interested in sharing that information. This kind of person is approached by many for advice, and will have many incoming connections that demonstrate the desire for information.
- The *salesman* has skills of both persuasion and negotiation, and may be positioned in the connectivity graph in a pivotal point that separates, yet bridges two communities.

There are many other potential roles that can be represented in the connectivity graph, and we can characterize how each role is defined in relation to some basic properties, such as the *distance* between any two actors in a network, the *degree* (or the number of edges attached to each actor), the *betweenness* (that measures how an actor lies on the critical path between other actors), as well as numerous other properties. Each contributes to a determination of how much influence any individual actor exerts within the environment, and each of the described roles exerts different types of influence among the communities that surround them. In other words, each archetypal role can be depended on to communicate messages in different ways across their sphere of influence.

THE ADVANTAGE OF UNDERSTANDING SPHERES OF INFLUENCE

The desire to model customer connectivity suggests the need for developing a representative graph/network model of the entities that act within a community and the relationships between and among those entities. The objectives of building this model include understanding the different influences exerted by key individuals within the network and consequently using that knowledge in communicating a message (such as "buy our product!") across that network.

The first step to this level of insight is reviewing the individuals associated with your customer community and identifying the different types of roles those individuals play. Each of these individuals can influence others in some way, and if you can strategically communicate your message to the right individual at the right time, you can exploit their spheres of influence.

To continue the example using Gladwell's roles: the maven may be linked to many others seeking his/her special knowledge. Providing those mavens with some inside scoops about special features in your upcoming products is one way to broadcast the awareness of those new features to the maven's followers. Engaging the connectors in a positive way will help in efficiently spreading the message quickly across the customer community. Lastly, the salesman can be engaged to advocate on behalf of the company to influence others to actually commit to purchasing the product.

SOCIAL NETWORK MEASURES FOR CUSTOMER CENTRICITY

The sphere of influence and the strength of that influence should be reflected in the social network model. That highlights the importance of the different graph metrics. These metrics are intended to provide some insight into the qualitative characteristics associated with linkages within and across the network.

For example, a good place to start is Wikipedia's page on social network analysis[1] that provides an interesting list of metrics that deserve further consideration to review how their measures can be interpreted for customer centricity (Table 5.1).

[1] See http://en.wikipedia.org/wiki/Social_network_analysis, downloaded on September 13, 2013.

Table 5.1 Some Examples of Network Analysis Metrics

Metric Name	Description	Interpretation for Customer Centricity
Distance	The number of edges between any two specific nodes.	Characterizes closeness of any pair of individuals.
Betweenness centrality	This measure is associated with a specific node in the graph, and quantifies the number of shortest paths from all nodes to any of the other nodes that pass the specific node.	Finds individuals who are near intersections of closer-knit subcommunities. These are individuals whose influence spans multiple groups, and are like "brokers."
Closeness centrality	This measure is associated with a specific node in the graph, and quantifies the average distance from that node to every other node in the network.	Finds individuals who are near the center of clusters, and indicates people who are well-known within a group and whose opinions are well-respected.
Eigenvector centrality	This measures the connectedness of any individual node to parts of the network that are highly connected, so finds individuals whose connections also have many connections.	This identifies influential individuals with connections to other influential individuals, but not necessarily the breadth implied by closeness.
Bridge	Identifies an individual providing the only link between two other subgraphs (either individuals or clusters).	Finds the key people for ensuring that a message can be transmitted across the breadth of the network.
Density	The ratio of direct connections in the network compared to the total possible number of direct connections.	Characterizes the degree to which the entire customer population is tightly connected.
Homophily	This measures the degree to which individuals with a set of characteristics are connected to others with similar characteristics.	This reflects the concept that "birds of a feather flock together," and helps find whether certain similarities exist across groups of connected customers.
Multiplexity	This measures the number of different links between any two nodes.	This helps find sets of customers that have a stronger or more closely knit connection, such as people who are related, work at the same company, and live in the same town.
Reciprocity	The degree to which two individuals mimic each other's sets of connections.	This can identify people who share a set of interests or friend but may not have explicitly connected with each other. This can help with suggestions for alignment with special interest groups.
Cliques	A clique is a group of individuals in which each one is connected to all others in the group.	This is useful for finding communities of interest that share similar interests together—good for driving recommendation engines.

These are a subset of the types of features or discoveries one might look for in a social network. In turn, they are all similar in that they map technical aspects of the representative network graph to behavioral or demographic aspects of real relationships and group dynamics.

CUSTOMER CONNECTIVITY MEASURES AND INFLUENCING THE SPHERES

Understanding the dynamics associated with the ways that individual customers interact within the context of different characteristic sub-communities can guide your company's methods of sharing information and generally positively impact the outcomes of communicating with any specific customer. This suggests blending the use of social network analysis and selected network metrics with your customer profile.

The goal is to leverage knowledge about a customer's roles within the community to increase overall value. For example, one customer may have a relatively low volume of sales, but within the customer community has a high measure of closeness centrality. That might imply that this customer is well-connected and well-known, and the customer's opinion is highly respected. Therefore, it might be a reasonable decision to ensure a positive experience at every touch point even if the immediate operational cost might seem to be high.

The reason is that the specific customer's experiences are likely to be shared among a broad spectrum of other individuals, potentially impacting their buying or retention decisions. A good experience for an influential customer translates to increased value, while a bad experience may result in reduced revenues and ultimately attrition. This means that it is reasonable to consider the incorporation of network measures as part of an overall customer valuation model and interaction strategy.

CHAPTER 6

Customer Touch Points and the Exchange of Value

UNDERSTANDING CUSTOMER INTERACTIONS

Chapter 3 examined the concept of "customer" along with the variety of meanings that the term "customer" takes on in different business contexts. After considering the challenges of creating a single definition of customer, though, we came to the conclusion that it might be worthwhile for organizations to recast the concept of "customer" in the context of the relationship between the organization and a customer. So instead of hyperfocusing on the semantics of the terminology, exploring ways to manage the different aspects of customer relationships will enhance the customer experience and eventually lead to increased profitability.

Essentially, the relationship with a customer is composed of the series of interactions between the company and the customer. Therefore, one approach to managing the different aspects of the relationship is to consider every interaction with any presumed customer entity (individual or organization) in which there is an exchange of value. We will refer to that as a *customer interaction*. The ability to consider all customer interactions relies on two fundamental ideas:

1. Your organization has the ability to effectively identify the scenarios within any business process where two entities interact and there is an identifiable exchange of value.
2. You are able to describe and quantify what that exchange of value is.

We can begin with an assessment of the business functions that are traditionally associated with customer interactions and their processes. For example, the marketing function seeks to attract and engage prospects, while the sales function looks to convert prospects into committed purchasers. There may be a fulfillment function tasked with the delivery of the purchased product or service, the finance function to collect payments, and a customer service function to deal with inquiries and complaints. Each of these business functions has some interaction with customers; the challenge is to identify (and document, if necessary) the business processes and then specify where in the process the customer interaction occurs.

The customer interaction can be divided into two components: what we will call the "touch point," or the method by which the interaction occurs, and the exchange of value. Once those customer interaction points are identified, they can be characterized in terms of the type of interaction and the categorization of the "value" that is exchanged between the two parties. In the next sections, we will discuss the different types of customer touch points, the different means of exchanging value, and then consider what information about the customer is needed for the analyses and guidance that can be used to augment those interactions in positive ways that become memorable and thereby increase customer lifetime longevity and value.

CUSTOMER SEGMENTATION INFLUENCES THE RELATIONSHIP

Customer-centric organizations adjust their lenses to operate from the perspective of the customer in building trust and loyalty by attempting to ensure that each of the customer's interactions is a positive experience. One of the major objectives is to encourage longer term retention, since retaining existing customers incurs much lower costs than new customer acquisition. In turn, existing customers whose trust and loyalty you have already gained are more likely to purchase something from your company than they are from a business with whom they have no experience.

Changing customer-facing business processes to enable building a customer's trust and loyalty depends on developing a profile of the customer that reflects how past interactions influence that customer's behavior. The information used to populate that profile can guide staff members involved in those business processes in the best ways to treat the customer in the way that provides an experience consistent with the customer's characteristics.

Developing many customer profiles allows you to perform the analyses that can identify the characteristics that similar types of customers share. These help you devise the basis of describing customer segments—groups of customers with shared characteristics who exhibit similar (and therefore predictable) behaviors under similar circumstances. Some examples include groups of customers living in the same geographic region, have similar educational background, and who have purchased products from a selected subset of your product catalog. Other examples include groupings of customers who purchase a certain set of products you have, or it may be groupings of customers who spend within specific dollar ranges each month, or groupings into different age ranges.

This process of identifying the categories and relative relevance and then placing customers in the proper grouping is called *segmentation*. Segmentation, which will be discussed in greater detail in Chapters 8 and 9, involves multivariate analysis in which a number of categories of interest are defined, and customers are then placed in the appropriate groupings for each category. Customer segmentation strategies can be used in two different ways: grouping and organizing customers and determining levels of engagement and treatment based on any customer's segment. Segmentation provides some valuable benefits, and some examples include:

- Helping a company achieve a better overall understanding of the types of customer the business serves.
- Help set the stage for more precise analysis of customer types.
- Guide customer support processes and advise representatives about levels of support based on customer value.

SEGMENTATION, CUSTOMER TOUCH POINTS, AND PERSONALIZATION

While some businesses have a limited use of customer segmentation and profiling, others actually take profiling a step further by trying to create unique experiences personalized for each customer. Instead of just dropping groups of similar customers into broad segments based on limited amounts of customer data, they attempt to build more sophisticated models and profiles that can drive direct personalization. When detailed customer data can be integrated into operational processes, your company can develop increasingly customer-centric experiences.

Both broad customer segmentation and unique personalization require the collection and management of data about the customer's characteristics (which are generally static attributes that do not change often or at all, such as date of birth or home address) and behavior (which is more likely to reflect dynamic attributes such as the products purchased or durations of customer support calls).

Both of these types of data attributes can be captured about a customer at points where the customer and the business interact—those same touch points introduced earlier in this chapter. Each touch point provides an opportunity to both learn more about each individual customer as well as employ what is already known to influence customer behaviors in ways that are valuable to both the customer and to your business. As an added benefit beyond growing each individual profile, data collected about each individual also contributes to the enrichment of the broader customer segments, which can inform more business processes and corresponding touch points to enhance the general customer experience.

A track record of positive experiences will have a cumulative effect in developing a rapport with the customer, strengthening trust in the business, and intensifying the customer's loyalty. The impact can be heightened when the details of the interactions within individual business process touch points can be tailored to unique customer profiles based on an analysis of a combination of characteristics and behavior data.

TYPES OF CUSTOMER TOUCH POINTS

Customer interactions may take place along a wide variety of touch points, of which each organization may employ some subset. Some of these touch points involve direct human–human interaction, such as when a customer talks to a bank teller inside a branch office. Human touch points suggest a level of intimacy with customers and may be perceived as good channels for establishing and developing personal customer relationships. Other touch points are automated, such as the use of a customer service app running on a smart mobile device or through interactive voice recognition systems supporting the inbound call process. A number of different types of touch points are described in Table 6.1.

Common examples of touch points include Point of Sale (POS), online store purchases, all activities associated with web site visits, numerous types of smartphone and other mobile device interactions

Table 6.1 Examples of Different Types of Touch Points

Touch Point	Example	Human/Nonhuman Interaction
Brick and Mortar POS	Purchasing food at a supermarket	Human
Online store POS	Electronics purchase from an online only vendor	Nonhuman
General web site visits	Searching for products from an online vendor	Nonhuman
Smartphone interactions	Travel delay alerts delivered to mobile device	Nonhuman
Self-service kiosks	Self checkout at the hardware store	Nonhuman
Coupon redemption	Use of a printed coupon at a Brick and Mortar location	Human
Coupon redemption	Use of a coupon code for online purchase	Nonhuman
Inbound call center customer service	Customer complaint	Human
Outbound call center processes	Sales call	Human
Survey interactions	Online marketing survey	Nonhuman
Email interactions	Notification of received payment	Nonhuman
Billing statements	Mailed invoice	Nonhuman
In-store merchandizing and promotions	"buy one get one free"	Nonhuman
Direct mail and Newsletters	Mailed advertisements	Nonhuman
Broad-based public communication	Press releases	Nonhuman
Advertising	Newspaper advertisements	Nonhuman
Social media (e.g., blogs, Facebook, Twitter)	Facebook "likes"	Nonhuman
Demonstrations	In-store demos	Human
Demonstrations	YouTube videos	Nonhuman
Product use	Customer experience utilizing product or service	Human
Product use	Customer experience utilizing product or service	Nonhuman

and applications, engagement via self-service kiosks, both inbound and outbound call center customer representative interactions, physical and virtual surveys, emails, "snail-mail" mailings, as well as a slew of others.

Interestingly, there are even nonobvious touch point methods that can be used to engage your customer in different ways, such as sounds

Figure 6.1 This guy[1] really makes me want to get a frankfurter.

and music piped through the store, pleasant odors pumped out to the street from a restaurant, visual cues incorporating signs, layout, and even mannerisms and gestures (see Figure 6.1).

Touch points have a "direction"—they can be considered to be bidirectional when they involve two entities (such as an in-store POS purchase) or unidirectional (such as mailed advertisements). Bidirectional touch points provide a means for engagement and data collection.

THOUGHTFUL COORDINATION OF CUSTOMER TOUCH POINTS

It is interesting to consider the different impacts on the customer relationship in the context of each of these touch points, especially when comparing human touch points to the nonhuman ones. Often, automation has been employed as a replacement for humans as way to help organizations scale up their operations while managing the costs associated with human staff resources. As a result, in many industries there

[1]"A Muffler Man holding a hot dog." Image authored by Mykl Roventine. Originally posted **Flickr** as Muffler Man with Hot Dog. Downloaded October 3, 2013 from http://en.wikipedia.org/wiki/File:Muffler_Man_with_Hot_Dog.jpg. This file is licensed under the Creative Commons Attribution 2.0 Generic license.

are far fewer human touch points today than there were in the past. The proliferation of nonhuman touch points emphasizes the importance of human touch points because the direct interaction often provides a more satisfying result. Direct contact may be the best way to build relationships with customers, especially when there is a concern that reduced human interactions can cause damage to a customer relationship.

Yet while there may be many nonhuman touch points, the organization's internal perspective may use them as means to an end—aspects of operational processes that operate solely within specific line of business functions. For example, a bank's mortgage business may provide an online portal for managing payments, while the same bank may also provide a mobile app for credit card accounts. Often the applications associated with each touch point are designed, developed, and implemented within a virtual silo with little or no cross-organizational coordination.

This lack of coordination means that the applications are solely designed to meet functional requirements and are probably not engineered to contribute to a holistic customer experience. And because the customers are more likely to be engaged through nonhuman touch points, your company should be aware of the potential negative impact of less than stellar experiences, as they will be compounded over time and diminish the customer's loyalty. This suggests that your company's strategy for customer centricity must include team members whose job is to oversee the quality, consistency, and interoperability of the numerous touch points, both human and nonhuman.

THE CONCEPTUAL EXCHANGE OF VALUE

The company's relationship with the customer is a two-way street, implying that every customer interaction and touch point involve an exchange of value between the company and the customer. An easily recognized example of value exchange occurs when a customer decides to buy a product from a company. In this scenario, the customer exchanges money (which has value) for the purchased product (which also has value).

The objective is to look at all customer interactions and be able to describe what that exchange of value entails—what does the customer get and what does the company get? Looking at some other use case scenarios helps in isolating the conceptual value that is being exchanged:

- *Customer complaint*, in which a customer engages the company's customer support team to complain about a product or service. The value that the customer is seeking is support or warranty for some perceived defect of the product or service. The value the company gains is an important feedback about the product that can be integrated into other support interactions or even fed back into the design and development cycle to improve the product.
- *Prospect query*, in which a prospective customer engages a salesperson for information about the product. The customer is seeking information or insight, with the value cast in terms of gaining knowledge about the product and the company. The salesperson is provided with qualifying information about the prospect, which is valuable as part of the salesperson's engagement and sales process.
- *Customer payment*, in which the customer provides money (which of course has value to the company) in return for settlement of the purchasing agreement and elimination of a payment obligation (which is valuable to the customer).

Note that in each of these cases there is an *exchange* of value—both parties get something out of the interaction. In some cases, the exchange is perceived to be even, such as exchanging money for a product. In other cases, the value one party receives is greater than that received by the other party.

More likely, in many cases the parity (or disparity) between exchange of value is not clear. Those areas of potential confusion represent opportunities—either look for ways to eliminate the disparity in exchange of value or seek to improve different aspects of the value exchange.

A good example is the last scenario we looked at: customer payment. The immediate perception is that the value of receiving a payment is much greater for the company than giving it is for the customer. This bears further review—perhaps the value is greater to the company the earlier the payment is made, and therefore an incentive might be given to a customer who pays ahead of schedule. And in fact it is not uncommon for agreements to include a discount for early payments.

Alternatively, the value to the customer is greater in eliminating a debt obligation faster, restoring a full line of credit, thereby allowing the customer to stock raw materials from its vendors at the same time. This presents an opportunity to the company—provide a discount on future sales as an incentive for early payment, which may influence the customer to employ the line of credit to sooner purchase more of the company's products.

The upshot is that reviewing business processes to identify the customer touch points and evaluating the exchange of value will expose opportunities for improvement that can be evaluated based on the context of the process and the identity of the parties involved.

ANALYZING TOUCH POINTS TO MAXIMIZE EXCHANGED VALUE

Needless to say, enhancing the customer experience is tightly coupled with the desire to maximize the exchange of value during each customer interaction. A basic approach to maximizing value might involve these steps:

- Cataloging all the customer touch points.
- Isolating the types and magnitude of the value exchanged.
- Prioritizing the touch points in terms of goals for increased value for all involved parties.
- Determining what information is needed to increase value.
- Determining the business processes to be updated to take advantage of that information.

Each of these tasks depends on a fundamental holistic understanding of how the different touch points reflect a corporate culture of customer interaction. To accomplish this, you need to inventory and catalog all the customer touch points as a prelude to identifying any lost opportunities, find any gaps in the customer interface, and importantly assign accountability for the success measures associated with each touch point. More directly, this means:

- Within each business process, identify all existing customer touch points.
- Identify the party within the organization who is responsible for the business process and for each touch point.

- Validate that each touch point has a specific purpose related to the anticipated outcome of the business process.
- Ensure that there are defined performance metrics associated with the expected outcomes and how each touch point contributes to that outcome.
- Use those performance metrics to baseline the current effectiveness of the business process and the contribution of each touch point.
- Specify performance goals for each touch point and consider how increasing exchanged value can impact those performance measures.
- Determine whether there are opportunities for expanding or reducing the number of touch points within the business process.
- Explore how to improve the business processes to maximize performance.

MAPPING THE CUSTOMER'S JOURNEY

While these steps may seem obvious, actually performing them can be quite complex and requires commitment throughout the organization. One approach is based on mapping the customer's journey through various usage scenarios. This approach puts the analyst in the shoes of the customers and provides the perspective of each interaction from the lens of a customer.

This approach can be augmented by creating multiple customer personas, each of which representing one of the different customer types. The role of the customer persona can be played by people within the company, or real customers can be engaged to walk through the simulation. When real customers are used, staff members must be available to observe the process.

When each customer persona traverses the journey, each touch point is revealed and can be documented. After each persona's journey is traversed, the results from all the simulations are then collected, sorted by touch point, and each touch point's owner is documented or assigned if one had not already been assigned. As the simulation becomes more sophisticated, the performance measures can be applied to assess how well each touch point achieved its objectives.

Touch point owners are responsible for reviewing the performance results for their assigned touch points. The owner examines current results with those from previous reviews to see the effect of applied improvements. This also provides a means for capturing suggestions and possible improvement once the magnitude of exchanged values are determined.

This review also may expose new opportunities for characterizing each touch point: is it human or nonhuman? Is it unidirectional or bidirectional? The assessment also helps in determining if the right data is being captured at each of the interactions and any dependencies among more than one touch point.

The exercise is repeated on a periodic cycle so that improvements to business processes and customer interactions can be measured. In turn, these periodic reviews help the analysts identify areas requiring further improvement, as well as identify any recently created touch points that might not have existed or inventoried in earlier iterations.

Don't be alarmed if the magnitude of this effort seems extreme. These assessments can be begun on a small scale by selecting specific business processes, customer journeys, and personas that are presumed to have significant influence on overall customer behavior. Over time, the analysis can expand breadthwise to include different business processes or depthwise to include more personas.

On the other hand, realize that the iterative nature of performing this analysis demands discipline and planning. It will require an investment in time and resources and therefore will require significant commitment at nearly all levels of the organization. Senior managers will need to make a particular commitment to ensure that those involved have the time and resources to engineer and perform these tasks.

CHAPTER 7

Organizing Data for Customer Centricity

CUSTOMER PROFILING AND CUSTOMER IDENTITY

In Chapter 6, we suggested that reviewing the exchanges of value at different customer touch points exposed opportunities for improvement, depending on the business processes and coincidental opportunities. All of these opportunities must be framed by who the customer is, what that customer likes and dislikes, and how that customer's decisions are influenced. This is more simply referred to as a customer profile, and the process of creating that profile is called customer profiling; this will be discussed in much greater detail in Chapter 8.

There are many different considerations and aspects of customer profiling. Most of these center on the relationship between the business context (such as a physical location, a set of virtual visits to web sites, or points in time, for example) coupled with the generalizations that can be made about interactions that take place within any of those specific contexts.

However, a specific customer's profile must encompass more than just context information regarding location or point in time. The most comprehensive models for customer profile blend different aspects of the decision-making processes presented to the customer, ranging from small decisions such as which links to click on a web site to large decisions such as committing to buying a product. Each decision presented to the customer results in a choice made, and the result of each of these decisions can be added to the profile. The more sophisticated analytical models can use this aggregated information about selected touch points and interactions to look for probabilities that certain kinds of decisions will be made at each future touch point.

The ability to take advantage of this analysis of aggregated histories associated with customer decision relies on the ability to develop your customer profiles and get access to information about any customer within any of the business contexts in order to inform the processes with better customer intelligence. Both building and delivering the customer profiles require effective approaches to accessing, integrating, organizing, and managing customer data; in this chapter, we look at some of the conventional wisdom for data organization.

THE NEED FOR DATA ORGANIZATION

The need for considering alternatives for organizing customer data for analysis is related to the fact that the conventional approach to data organization within a business is largely correlated to the original operational intent. For example, customer data is collected as part of a sales function to ensure that the transaction can be completed, the customer is properly charged, and the product can be delivered. Once the transaction is completed, the need for the customer data is filled.

Generally, whether customer data is collected or created as a result of executing a business transaction or managing operational activities, that information is effectively a byproduct of the transaction or operation. In turn, the "management" of that data is limited to archiving— capturing the record of the event and maintaining it in case someone needs to examine it in the future.

However, in an organization that plans to adopt a customer-centric strategy, that same data seen as a byproduct of operational processing becomes a critical asset. The challenge, though, is that the typical approaches to organizing data for transaction processing are not necessarily suited to analytical processing, for a number of reasons, such as:

- The quality of the data is sufficient for the execution of the transaction but may not be satisfactory for the analysis.
- The underlying models may not capture the desired data attributes that are needed to profile the customers.
- The level of precision in identifying customers uniquely is not relevant to the transaction processing and fulfillment processes.
- Demographic data to be used for analysis may not be needed to execute the transaction.
- Information about relationships, connectivity, and conceptual hierarchies is not needed for transaction completion.

COLLECTING KEY DATA ARTIFACTS

Customer profiles employed within a customer centricity strategy rely on some key data artifacts organized in a way that supports the analyses that segment, characterize, classify, and group customer data. This means that from the beginning, the analysis is going to require organization of customer data along specific facets, including:

- **Entity and identity data**, which first enables you to define a specific representative model for a customer and then select those attributes that can be used to uniquely differentiate any specific customer from all others.
- **Attribution data**, which are the variables that can ultimately be used as part of the analysis for clustering, segmentation, and classification.
- **Relationship data**, comprising logical groupings (such as a "household"), hierarchies (such as a company's org chart), and relationships (such as a social network).
- **Behavior data**, consisting of the collected sets of transactions, interactions, and even the reactions that take place at the different customer touch points.

These four categories provide the basis for developing an analytical customer profile.

ORGANIZING ENTITY AND IDENTITY DATA

Almost by definition, a customer-centric strategy demands identification of each unique customer within the customer community. Creating a representative model of the customer is a necessary prelude to developing customer profile models and analyzing any characteristics and behaviors for classification. That model must, at the very least, incorporate these aspects:

- **Description of the entity**, namely an explanation of what the business roles are for the represented entity, how those roles are manifested within business processes, and how those roles are distinguished within the community. For example, there may be a concept of a "head of household customer." That role is relevant as long as there is a description of that role's business meaning, such as "the individual who is responsible for payment for a provided service." There may be affiliated roles as well, such as "household member" customers who do not have financial accountability but are eligible for customer service.
- **Identifying characteristics**, which comprise the collected set of data attributes that can be used to uniquely distinguish one customer

from another. An example of a set of identifying characteristics might be first name, last name, date of birth, city of birth, and state of birth. In addition, there should be a way of differentiating identifying characteristics from the behavioral or descriptive characteristics that will contribute to the customer analysis. These are typically the data elements whose data values are inherent to the individual.

- **Unique identifier**, which is a key value that is associated with one and only one customer.
- **Methods for recognizing entity information**, which are critical in dissecting individual data embedded within semi-structured data or for recognizing entity information embedded within unstructured data. As an example, account-oriented data models often subsumed multiple identities associated with a single bank account's name, such as "Mr. and Mrs. John Franklin UGMA John Franklin Jr." In this case, there are three unique individuals referenced in the account name: Mr. John Franklin, Mrs. John Franklin, and John Franklin Jr., along with a reference to a financial vehicle that relates those three individuals.
- **Methods for resolving unique identity**, which become necessary as the customer community expands. Initial attempts at determining identifying attributes may work well until the pool of individuals expands to include people who share their set of identifying attribute values. At that point, a process must be used to differentiate between two real-world entities that share the same set of identifying attributes. This may require the augmentation of the set of identifying characteristics, which may require a recalculation/repopulation of the customer data set.
- **A customer entity data model**. This model must not only be able to capture the identifying characteristics but also enable both linkage with additional entity data (such as locations or contact mechanisms) and subsume relationship and hierarchy connections that are used to help evaluate any individual customer's sphere of influence.

MANAGING CUSTOMER ATTRIBUTION AND CLASSIFICATION DATA

There is a difference between data attributes used for unique identification and those used for attribution to facilitate customer segmentation and classification. An example of some attributes used for segmentation are those associated with location, such as home address, or package delivery address, or those associated with time, such as the starting date of a provided service. A customer's home address can be combined with regional profiles of purchasing patterns of other individuals living nearby and that can guide your company's decisions of the types of products or promotions to offer customers of the same ilk.

In other words, attribution elements are those data elements whose values can be used for generally describing pools of individuals. These attributes contribute to describing a cluster or a segment, as well as those data elements that can drive the iterative analysis of customer clusters and segments. A good example is sex/age groupings used for media analytics, such as "males between the ages of 18 and 34." In general, these demographic data elements are descriptive and span the range of geographic, psychographic, and historical data elements. Some more discrete examples include location of birth, number of cars owned, level of education attainment, net worth, home ownership, etc.

In some cases, attribution data elements are inherent to the individual and do not change (such as location of birth), while others can change over time (such as the customer's employer). Inherent data elements can be added to the core customer entity data model. However, you may want to manage multiple sets of attribution data elements (such as a permanent residence as well as a vacation residence) as well as track the history of more transient attribution relationships (such as maintaining the customer's employment history). In turn, each of these attribution elements might represent their own entities (such as a location, an organization, or a contact mechanism).

This suggests that one approach to organizing attribution data is to first determine whether any of those associated attributes are individual data elements or if they are entities in their own right. If they are individual data elements, they can be directly added to the customer entity model. Otherwise, the new entity concepts (such as "employer") can be modeled independently. In turn, each unique customer can be conceptually linked to these attribution entities in ways that capture both the association and the duration of the association.

LAYERING RELATIONSHIPS AND HIERARCHIES FOR CUSTOMER DATA ORGANIZATION

In Chapter 5, we discussed how a key concept of customer centricity is mapping relationship networks to assess any individual's sphere of influence. To support this type of analysis, it is critical that the organization of the data incorporate two different aspects of these networks.

The first is the concept of a *relationship*, which can bind a customer to some other entity or two customers together. We have already considered ways that one customer can be linked to other entities, such as an employer, a place of residence, or a contact mechanism. However, there is a qualitative difference between the knowledge that can be derived from those types of relationships and the relationships between and among customers themselves.

Because the interaction of social networks that effectively self-organize within a customer community shed light on aspects of a customer's profile in terms of communal likes and dislikes within a subgroup, recommendation engines often rely on connection networks to help refine suggestions and promotions. Yet more complex networks are difficult to represent using a standard relational model, so different paradigms (such as graph models) may be better suited to organizing customer connectivity networks.

The second aspect of connectivity looks at *hierarchical organization* instead of examining links between peers. As an example, we can revisit the concept of a "household," which links a group of individuals together based on similar characteristics and under the guidance or control of a hierarchy of individuals. One manifestation of a household is a "traditional family," in which one or two adults oversee a collection of children living in the same location. Another manifestation might be a special interest group of individuals sharing some common interests (such as a motorcycle club) led by an elected set of officials.

The organization of hierarchy data is similar to that of standard relationships plus the addition of a "direction" or "inclusion" within the model. Members of that special interest group are linked together in a way that documents the interest, and individuals with leadership roles need to be organized by their level of influence (e.g., the president of the club can be seen above the vice president in the conceptual hierarchy). Again, the relational model may not work as well as a directed graph model might, since the latter might be able to capture both the connections and the hierarchical levels.

ORGANIZING CUSTOMER BEHAVIOR DATA

Organizing aspects and characteristics of customers and their connections is relatively straightforward when compared to organizing and managing behavior data. First of all, a "behavior" is an action an individual takes when presented with a set of alternatives. For example, a customer entering a clothing store is presented with a wide alternative of articles of clothing to purchase. That customer might either purchase one or more articles, or decide not to buy any of them.

Behavior data poses somewhat of a challenge unless it can be discretely described, represented, and managed. There are different kinds of behaviors associated with different types of decision-making scenarios, each with its own variety of alternatives. The data organization approaches span a spectrum. At one end, the data captured for each scenario is very granular, capturing the context of the decision, the alternatives, and the actual decision made. This side of the spectrum requires dedicated design and engineering, and the actual amount of information collected may be very great.

To use our clothing store, for example, that means capturing a full enumeration of the entire store's shelf stock and logging what each customer did, each time a customer entered a store. And while this may sound like overkill, the need for collecting massive amounts of data created at decision points is becoming more commonplace. For example, similar scenarios are captured on a routine basis for e-commerce sites, in which a variety of products are presented to a web site visitor, and the specific actions (such as which products are clicked on, how long the visitor spent on each page, the sequence of clicks, etc.) are scrupulously captured and potentially positioned for later analysis.

At the other end of the spectrum, similar scenarios can be absorbed into more abstract entities and more likely represent "predispositions" rather than discrete decisions. Again, using the clothing store, the gross-level behavior can be boiled down into two alternatives: the customer entered the store and either bought something or bought nothing. The loss of granularity reduces the amount of data that must be captured and stored, but perhaps at the sacrifice of more precise information for later analysis.

No matter which end of the spectrum is considered, the data that comprises what is represented as a behavior can be linked to a customer with its corresponding context—the location (either real or virtual), the time, the duration, along with the details of the alternatives, and the final decision.

MANAGING CUSTOMER IDENTITY

The considerations of data organization for customer centricity point toward the need for more formal approaches for both analyzing customer behavior at particular contextual interactions and subsequently informing decision scenarios using data pulled from customer profiles. But if the focal point is the knowledge from the profile that influences behavior, you must be able to recognize the individual, rapidly access that individual's profile, and then feed the data from the profile into the right analytical models that can help increase value.

The biggest issue is the natural variance in customer data collected at different touch points in different processes for different business functions. For example, a business executive may be referred to more formally using a title and full first and last names ("Mr. Jeffrey Johnson"). But that same individual may be referred to less formally when socializing among friends ("Jeff Johnson"). The multitude of interfaces in which an individual's name is collected may lead to numerous variations across many different data sets. A search for the exact representation provided may not always result in a match, and at worse, may lead to the creation of new records for the same individual, even if one or potentially more records already exist.

In the best scenario, the ability to rapidly access the customer's profile is enabled through the combination of intelligent name matching routines that are tolerant to some variance along with the creation of a master index. That master index contains the right amount of identifying information about customers to be able to link two similar records together when they can be determined to represent the same individual while differentiating records that do not represent the same individual. Once the right record is found in the index, a pointer can be followed to various data sets that contain the customer profile information.

The approach for indexing and searching, which most recently has taken on the name of "identity resolution," actually refers to matching and linkage techniques that have been available for many years in data quality and data cleansing tools, particularly those suited to customer data integration for direct marketing, mergers, acquisitions, data warehousing, and other cross-enterprise consolidation. In other words, the capability for developing customer data sets, the corresponding customer profiles, and integrated analytics builds on a level of matching and linkage competency that may already be established within the organization.

CUSTOMER PROFILE MODELING: SOME LAST CONSIDERATIONS

It is valuable to remember that even though the organization of customer data is predicated on the access, collection, and integration of identity, attribution, relationship, and behavioral data pulled from different source data sets, the intent of the customer profile is for consumption by analytics processes as well as downstream business users.

If the process is perceived to be about data consolidation, one might infer that the important aspects of the creation of the customer profile are data collection and distillation into a single "conformed" customer record. But as we have discussed, variations will exist across the different data sources, and each will have its own idiosyncrasies, attribution, and representations. Satisfying the need for consolidation means that the target model has to be robust enough to capture all the data but that can also lead to inconsistencies in the customer data sets and consequently challenges in merging data sets with variations. With this approach, the objective is the creation of the profile but not necessarily maximizing the value of *using* that profile.

As long as you recall that the intent for the customer profile is sharing information to inform business processes, the creation of customer profiles is really just a means to an end. The customer profile model is essentially the conduit through which the analytics team analyzes customer data and the business community accesses the customer data. Work together with your technical and data management teams to engineer a solid customer profile data model and that the design supports the assurance of high-quality data, resulting in greater confidence in the analytical results.

CHAPTER 8

Customer Profiling

INTRODUCTION

In Chapter 2, we introduced the concept of customer value; and in subsequent chapters, we have considered different aspects about knowledge of your customers as an important ingredient in executing a strategy for customer centricity. Knowing as much as possible about customers allows your company to continue to strengthen relationships with those customers and to build their trust. It also allows you to better understand their holistic needs and offer/upsell products and services that make your company the one vendor they look to in order to meet their overall needs.

One key aspect of the customer-centric strategy is categorizing and segmenting customers along different dimensions. For example, categorizing customers enables organizations to identify who they consider to be their "best customers." At the same time, this enables you to find customers who fall into defined categories by virtue of matching customer attributes against recognized profiles. This highlights the criticality of understanding the customer touch points and interactions. Adjusting your business processes to inform decision-making at the different customer interactions help the organization provide a more personalized customer experience that results in building customer loyalty.

Much of this depends on the process of building customer profiles: analysis, segmentation, and classification. This chapter introduces some of these ideas and examines the importance of profiling in the context of being able to take advantage of customer information to create or grow value.

WHAT IS CUSTOMER PROFILING?

Customer profiling refers to processes for capturing data about customers, analyzing that data to create information about customer behaviors, likes/dislikes, and other characteristics, and the presentation of that information to decision-makers in various customer-facing processes to promote profitable actions. The various customer characteristic values are combined and used to segment groups within the customer population in different ways related to expected customer behaviors. A simple example uses gender to divide the population into males and females, allowing the analysts to analyze different purchasing patterns based on gender. If there are significant differences in those patterns, it might warrant changes to customer interactions depending on whether the customer is male or female.

More generally put, customer segmentation is a modeling exercise that incorporates the methods for:

- Deciding on the set of customer attributes that might be relevant to include in an analysis.
- Analyzing the data and isolating the dependent attribute.
- Organizing the customer population by differentiation using those dependent attribute values.
- Classifying those segments in relation to expected business behavior.
- Using the segmentation model to classify customers.

Some examples are given in Table 8.1.

This model allows the analysts and the business subject matter experts to develop the protocols for treating the customers within the different segments differently to achieve different business goals. In turn, business guidance and decision processes prompting different

Table 8.1 Examples of Using Customer Segmentation		
Business Goal	Attributes	Example Use Case
Better targeted marketing	Age, gender	Segment all customers by gender and age, identify the males between the ages 30 and 40, analyze how much those customers spend on average, and decide whether modifications to the approach for marketing to that cohort would increase the customer segment's average monthly spend.
Reinforce loyalty and retention	Age, duration	Identify "long-time" customers whose average sales have tailed off over a recent time frame to offer discounts for "coming back."
Eliminate poorly performing customers	Average spend, duration, net worth	Find customers that incur recurring costs but do not generate a profitable revenue stream and impose a monthly service fee.
VIP service	Net worth, average monthly spend	Identify "high-net worth" customers and provide faster response at the call center.

actions could be more sophisticated and complex depending on the anticipated outcome. Profiling information can also be used at customer touch points to personalize the interaction based upon the known characteristics about the customer and help build customer loyalty. The profiling process can also be used in a proactive manner: based on information gleaned from customer profiling and segmentation, a business may decide to discontinue pursuing or marketing to certain customer segments.

PROFILING CHARACTERISTICS

Customer profiling generally depends on three types of data:

1. **Demographic** attributes, which are those that are typically used to describe individual entities within a population. These attributes can be combined to characterize the makeup of groups within a population. Some examples of demographic data concepts include age, gender, ethnicity, country of origin, race, marital status, education level, income level, dwelling type, number of adults in a household, number of children in household, or number of cars owned.
2. **Psychographic** attributes, which are those that describe acquired qualitative aspects of an entity. For people, examples may include attributes associated with personality ("she is a happy person"), opinions ("libertarian"), beliefs ("believes in astrology"), interests ("likes to mountain bike"), lifestyle ("wealthy"), likes, and dislikes. Psychographic information can often be inferred from one or multiple demographic traits.
3. **Behavioral** attributes, which are those attributes associated with assessment of historical data that reflects common patterns. Examples include product usage patterns, purchasing frequency, purchasing volume, or purchasing certain products together.

It is reasonable to assume that an organization developing a customer-centric strategy would look to modeling and collecting a variety and a combination of these different kinds of attributes.

DESCRIBING SEGMENTS

Customer segments can be organized around any of these types of attributes. For example, a demographic segment might include all female customers between the ages of 20 and 30 who are married and have two or more children. Simple examples of psychographic segments could be customers who like golf, like classical music, drive luxury vehicles, or like to gamble. Behavioral segment examples include those who are frequent purchasers or people who call customer support more than twice a week.

Customer segments become more interesting when they are based on a combination of demographic, psychographic, and behavioral attributes. An example might be female customers between the ages of 20 and 30 with two or more children and who like golf and drive a luxury vehicle and call customer support more than twice a week.

Sometimes there are explicit or implicit dependencies and relationships among different sets of attributes. Certain psychographic attributes may be correlated to certain demographic attributes. For example, a cohort of male customers between the ages of 40 and 60 with high levels of income may drive luxury cars. While one's first reaction might be to presume some inherent relationship to the correlation ("males having a mid-life crisis with financial means will buy sports or luxury cars"), you must remember that correlation does not imply causality.

Just because a correlation is noted does not necessarily mean that one set of attribute values caused some behavior. On the other hand, the existence of the correlation can lead you to make certain decisions, such as researching the correlation to determine if there is a causal relationship, and perhaps to adjust your business processes as a result of noting the correlation. For example, luxury car dealerships could use our example correlation to attempt to appeal to existing or potential customers within that segment with specific targeted messaging.

CUSTOMER DATA ACQUISITION

Customer profiling requires the collection and acquisition of the data as well as the analysis of that information. Demographic, psychographic, or product usage data about customers can be acquired through a number of means.

As suggested in Chapter 6, customer touch points and interactions are fruitful sources for collecting demographic, psychographic, and behavioral data. A common example involves asking customers for their phone number, email address, or zip code at the point of purchase. Another example is the incremental accumulation of data that can be used to formulate behavioral attributes, such as the frequency of purchases.

Not all customer data needs to be accumulated from internal sources. There are many companies that are data aggregators: they have amassed and acquired large amounts of customer data, often from numerous sources and providers, and package that data into formats that are more easily absorbed. For example, some aggregators sell selected data sets of individuals who exhibit certain demographic or psychographic characteristics, such as all pharmacists who practice in a particular geographic region. In many cases, there is collaboration among different data providers, and some may engage their own customers and acquire their data sets, enrich them through integration with other data sets, and then sell it right back to those same customers!

This last point does raise the question about protection of customer data. The constraints are often covered within published privacy policies, but adherence to these policies may require some degree of caution to ensure against breaches of privacy.

PROFILING AND PERSONAS

While customer profiling may not be top of mind during a company's start-up phase, more sophisticated entrepreneurs and successful business entities use profiling as part of their business planning. Marketing managers will seek to understand their target customer and then plan around a customer profile and identify the types of products to sell based on the characteristics about the different customer segments they intend to target.

This approach can help in assessing the size of the market, determining market share, as well as even determining the customer "wallet share"—the amount of a customer's spend that is dedicated to the company's products and services. These measures can help the business identify strategies for capturing a greater percentage of the target audience as well as increasing the wallet share.

One way to begin the profiling process is to speculate about the characteristics of the potential customer types or "personas." The first step is to describe the personalities and other characteristics of the types of individuals they anticipate to be the most interested in the company's products or services. These characteristics are then expressed in demographic, psychographic, and behavioral criteria.

The next step would be to compare the existing customer base to the defined personas and to see how well the customers' attribute values and the persona values match. Discrepancies may indicate the need for some tweaking to the personas or may suggest that there are needs to make appropriate adjustments to the business processes. And, as we mentioned in Chapter 6, this highlights the criticality of mapping, understanding, and managing customer touch points and interactions. Touch points provide businesses with an opportunity to learn about individual customers while simultaneously collecting data that can contribute to the development of segmentation profiles and personas.

USING CUSTOMER PROFILES

Profile and persona information can be used to help the business validate that the consumers of their products or services are in fact the target audience they had intended to reach. After validating the existing customer base against the different personas, the next step is to use the profiling process to identify opportunities for customer centricity that might have been inadvertently ignored in the past. For example, once a customer persona has been validated, the characteristics of that person can define segmentation criteria to help identify existing customers with whom the relationship can be grown or prospective customers that can be directly contacted with specific offers.

There are a number of example use cases involving reviewing personas, transaction histories, and characteristic behaviors, such as using a recommendation engine: Examine historical information of individual customers that meet a profile and compare those to the larger group of customers meeting the profile. This allows you to identify any products or services commonly purchased by group members which are not purchased by specific individuals. These products can be recommended to the individual customer. Online book stores are known to make recommendations or suggestions based upon the purchases of others who have purchased books having a similar theme.

Profile transaction information can also be used by the business to identify patterns and see if there are implicit product bundles— combinations of products are often purchased together by members of a community or by individuals within a customer segment. For example, customers who have expressed an interest in a particular subject may purchase a variety of books related to that subject (e.g., a particular type of cooking). Identifying customers who have expressed an interest in that particular topic can help the organization in identifying the best book on that subject that they should be suggesting to other customers with similar interests.

In turn, the company can provide incentives to potentially interested customers to purchase the package by offering the combination of related products for a discount. This cross-selling opportunity is a good example of the exchange of value discussed in Chapter 6: The customer is provided with discounts for purchasing more items of interest, while the company can increase profitability by reduced shipping costs (when the items are shipped together) and more rapid product turnaround.

USE CASE: IMPROVING MARKETING EFFECTIVENESS

Customer profiling and analysis provides a business with insights enabling the business to define competitive and enticing packages to their customers. This can influence changes in business processes such as a company's marketing strategy. Marketing and product promotional strategies can be adjusted to each customer segment enabling optimization along dimensions such as reduced costs by marketing to more precise audiences through different types of media channels and enhancing the response rates from the target audiences.

By identifying characteristics about the customers that they intend to target or characteristics about existing customers, people in the organization can ensure that they are marketing and promoting their products through channels that target the customer base. And by collecting and analyzing customer profile data, the marketing organization can more easily identify the best suited channel types (e.g., websites, online or print magazines, television) that are visited, read, or viewed by the company's product or service consumers.

As a result of performing profile data analysis, a company may use the generated profiles to recognize they have different customer types that are sensitive to different marketing channels. They can use different marketing channels with separate targeted advertising messaging to most suitably resonate with each targeted customer group. This approach enables organizations to provide a more personalized experience as part of a customer-centric strategy by sending the right message at the right time to individuals within each particular audience.

Additionally, analyses of customer profile data can be used by marketing to measure the results of a new marketing campaigns intended to target new customer types. When profile information is effectively collected and analyzed, results of the analysis should help provide visibility to whether there is an increase in customers meeting the profile of the intended audience.

CONSIDERATIONS OF PRIVACY AND CHALLENGES OF CUSTOMER PROFILING

The benefits of collecting customer information are accompanied by some responsibilities as well. Consumers have come to expect a right to privacy, and that the data collected is to be used for very specific purposes. Yet customer data has been used for business advantage for many years, and it is only recently that the ability to analyze that data has become more apparent. There are some policies put in place to make the customers aware of how their data is being used.

For example, many websites provide privacy policies that describe the terms of use that include clauses delineating accountability for privacy and how collected data is used. People often do not read these clauses and do not understand that not only is their data being used for analysis within the company's domain, it is very likely that aggregated data is being packaged and sold to other organizations.

Companies may protect themselves legally by having customers click a box acknowledging they understand the use terms and conditions. However, increasing precision and accuracy of customer profiling can be perceived in a negative way when there is an implication that the company has drawn conclusions that "spook" the customer in some way. Ungoverned use of collected data and created profiles could backfire and damage trust and loyalty. Take this into consideration when scoping your customer analysis and profiling program.

TAKING CUSTOMER PROFILING TO THE NEXT LEVEL

Here are some ideas for jump-starting and expanding your company's customer profiling program:

- Define one or multiple personas for the types of customers you believe you are targeting. Specify the distinct and relevant characteristics for each persona you have defined that you would expect your customers to have.
- Define criteria for identifying what you consider to be your "best customers." Use these attributes to segment your customer base and identify the customers who fall into the "best customer" category.
- Map the customer touch points in some selected business processes. Augment your touch points to collect information about your customers, specifically information to determine profile characteristics. If so, verify that you are able to determine whether your customers meet the profile characteristics of your predefined personas.
- Consider the best marketing and promotional channels to target the customers who have the characteristics of your "best customers." Determine if you are effectively marketing through those channels.

These experiments can help you see if your company is missing opportunities for enhancing the exchange of value. In the next chapter, we will introduce some technical methods for customer analytics.

CHAPTER 9

Customer Data Analytics

THE ANALYTICS FEEDBACK LOOP

Many people often get the false impression that customer data analysis will indubitably result in the creation of value via a customer-centric strategy. But the reality is that there are two prerequisites for this to occur:

1. Understanding how the analysis supports the business opportunities for creating value.
2. Managing change in the organization to take best advantage of the analytical results.

In this chapter, we look at the first prerequisite in the context of describing analytical algorithms, while the second is treated in Chapter 10. However, the intent of both of these directives can be encapsulated in a straightforward sequence of tasks that can be replicated over and again for each business opportunity:

- **Identify the business problem** that must be solved, based on some awareness of an opportunity coupled with the desire to take advantage of the opportunity. These opportunities can be driven by the aspects of value discussed in Chapter 2, such as identifying opportunities for increasing revenue or reducing operating costs. You can frame the types of analyses to be performed when the objective is stated with specific details about the type of value, how it is to be created, and how it can be measured within a specific time period. An example might be "increase same-customer sales for the Southwest Region by 10% over the next 3 months."
- **Analyze the data**. Different techniques can be used to develop segmentation methods as well as predictive models that use those segments. This step includes data collection, organization, data and platform preparation (if necessary), analysis, testing/validation, and interpretation of the results to determine whether the analysis delivered actionable knowledge. If so, suggest alternatives that can be integrated within existing business processes or create new business

processes to test the hypothesis that the business objective can be met by executing those suggested changes.

- **Take the actions** suggested by the discoveries during the analysis process. Augment the existing process touch points by enhancing the customer interactions and informing the decision-makers. Track the decisions that are made and the actions that are taken for comparative purposes.
- **Measure results** to assess the degree to which the informed business process modifications addressed the original stated objectives. Compare the actual responses to the enhancements in the customer interactions and monitor the degree to which each change impacted the ultimate result.

Positive impacts can be reinforced by moving them into general production, while negative impacts indicate that the changes made were not adequate to affect the desired outcomes. Either way, this sequence can be restarted for the same business objective (but looking at different types of analyses) or could be initiated for other business opportunities.

CUSTOMER SEGMENTATION AND CLASSIFICATION

A large part of the analysis driving customer centricity is the ability to segment the customer population, to specify how those segments are characterized as categories or classes, and to use that knowledge to refine the customer interactions at the varied touch points.

Customer segmentation is a process that examines selected characteristics of an individual customer to provide some insight about the ways that customers with similar characteristics will behave in certain business scenarios. In the best situations, the determination of a customer's segment will inform the operational business processes in influencing the customer to make choices that lead to a result that is both desired by the company and beneficial to the customer. A simple example would involve segmenting customers by age groups, such as 18–34, 35–50, 50 and older, with the intent of customizing the presentation of marketing material and offers based on presumptions about individual preferences influenced by age.

SUPERVISED ANALYSIS

There are two basic approaches to employing analytic techniques for customer classification: categorization, and segmentation. When using a **supervised** approach, the analysts make presumptions about the pre-dispositions, preferences, or desires of individuals within a group based on research. Another way of looking at supervised or directed analysis is suggesting that you are aware of the problem to be solved and are using the analytics algorithms to find suspected relationships among a set of customer data variables that can help solve the problem.

The approach is "supervised" because the analysts already have some hypotheses they are looking to test and validate, such as "younger people buy more boxes of diapers." They will select the specific dependent variable ("number of boxes of diapers purchased") and they may direct the selection of potential independent variables (age groupings).

The more precise the hypothesis, the simpler it is to test by making specific queries and comparing the answers. If the hypothesis were "Customers that are 25 purchase more diapers than customers who are 49," then two queries could be executed: one tallying the count of sold diaper boxes when the customer age is 25 and one tallying the count of sold diaper boxes when the customer age is 49.

The challenge is when the hypothesis is less precise, and the question changes somewhat. Instead of a direct comparison of sales volume by specific age, the analyst might want to look at the corresponding sales volumes by customer ages from 18 to 65, examining the trends, and identifying the customer age bands based on levels of diaper sales. The resulting bands are the segments for diaper marketing based on the specific independent variable (in this case "age").

Additional characteristics can be layered into the segment as candidate independent variables to see if they impact the results, such as gender, geographic location, and/or income level. If these variables do affect the purchasing trends, their relative impacts can be folded into the business processes and marketing campaigns with more precise targeting.

The benefit of this supervised approach is that the analysts retain some level of control over the selection of what they believe to be are the independent variables. That selection provides some level of guidance as to the steps to take after the analyses are done, specifically in adjusting the business process or campaigns in reaction to what was learned.

UNSUPERVISED ANALYSIS

The second approach is **unsupervised**, in which the analysis is not predicated on the use of predetermined variables. In this undirected approach, the analysis is expected to reveal patterns within a data set that highlight some potentially interesting aspects of known entities and for exposing new potential opportunities. One distinction between the supervised and unsupervised approaches is that the unsupervised methods are more likely to uncover hidden behaviors and relationships, while the supervised methods can help in explaining and validating hypothesized relationships and patterns.

While the dependent variable may still be asserted, the customers to be segmented are subjected (along with a full complement of attributes) to one or more clustering algorithms that attempt to create the groups. In some cases, the algorithm is told the number of groups to create. In many cases, the analysts must review the decisions made by the algorithms to assign a customer into a particular group in relation to the proposed independent variables and their specific values (or value ranges). The algorithms iteratively formulate groups based on a proposed set of attribute values; after each iteration the groups are evaluated to assess their "stability," which might be measured in terms of the sensitivity of the assignment of a customer to a particular group if one of the attribute variables is slightly changed.

The benefit of the unsupervised approach is that it may uncover latent patterns and dependencies that are "interesting" in that they can motivate evaluation of opportunities for business advantage. An example might be discovering a small yet discretely discernable segment of individuals over the age of 50 that buy a significant number of boxes of diapers. The logical next step would be to evaluate the potential root causes or motivating factors associated with that cohort (such as "they are grandparents with custodial responsibility for their grandchildren") and determine whether what you can learn about the cohort can be used to create specialized customer engagement touch points for members of that cohort.

Both approaches to customer classification are valid and can add value, yet still require engagement with the business process owners to ensure that actions can be taken in relation to what is learned. One good way to examine the potential benefits of a comprehensive customer segmentation program is to start simple: begin with supervised analyses and gradually expand the program in terms of analytics flexibility and capability. Ensure that your business partners are engaged with the program and that pilot business activities can be designed and executed to provide proper testing and validation of the results.

ANALYSIS TECHNIQUES AND METHODS

Segmentation and classification are the cornerstones of customer-centric analysis, and it is worth examining the algorithmic methods applied to pull back the curtain somewhat and make the process less opaque to the business client. Here, we examine a number of common analysis techniques that can lead to the discovery of actionable knowledge:

- *Clustering* is the process that powers customer segmentation—it consumes the customer data sets and divides it into smaller groups in which each group's members exhibit some similarity. Clustering may dovetail with other analyses for identifying and potentially addressing business challenges, such as trying to determine the root cause of low sales within a particular market segment. Clustering can be extremely useful when you are not really sure what you are looking for but want to perform some kind of segmentation. The task of clustering involves the collection of data, initial distribution and grouping based on clear differentiating variables, and then iterative reorganization based on additional refinement from added-on variables. Different algorithms weigh different factors in the order of choosing the added-on variables, ranging from statistical variation to input from subject matter experts, who can help in refining the set of variables used as input (Figure 9.1).
- *Classification* is the process that follows clustering, and uses the values of identified dependent variables for organizing the customer population into predefined classes. There is a difference between clustering and classification: during the clustering task, the classes are not defined beforehand, and it is the process of evaluating the classes after the clustering has completed that drives the determination or definition of that class. Those selected variables and their value ranges are used as a model for organizing the existing customer community as well as determining the class to which new customers are added (Figure 9.2).

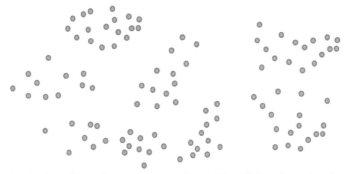

A collection of records are represented as entities within a dimensional space

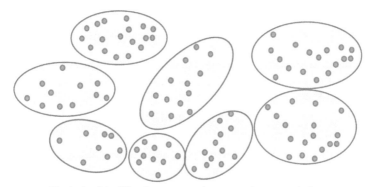

Clustering identifies the groups whose members are similar

Figure 9.1 Example of clustering.

- *Estimation* is a process of assigning some valued numeric value to an entity that can be used as part of a decision process. Typically, these scores are based on a continuous scale so that they can be compared and ranked. An example might score a customer's predisposition to purchasing a particular class of products. Estimation can use the results of a clustering and classification process, or might even be incorporated directly into a classification process. Estimation provides input about a customer's propensity to take some action, and the combination of classification and estimation provides the context for augmenting decision processes at customer touch points.
- *Prediction* models use classification and estimation together to classify objects according to some predicted anticipated future behavior. The use of historical data for considering how customers in different classes responded to specific offers or decisions can be used to train

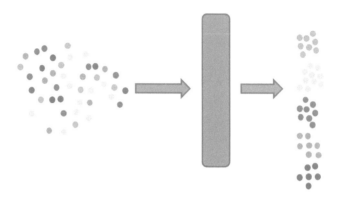

Figure 9.2 Classification of records based on defined characteristics.

a prediction model that can be directly integrated with customer interactions and guide the presentation of choice based on the predictive model.

- *Affinity grouping* is a process of evaluating relationships or associations between data elements that demonstrate some kind of affinity or connectivity between customers, such as grouping customers with certain psychographic attributes that have made certain product purchases. Marketing and sales campaigns for cross-selling and upselling can benefit from affinity grouping in different ways, such as creating different product bundles targeted at different customer segments.
- *Description* is the process of characterizing discovered results, assigning business value, and integrating those results into business processes as well as feeding those results into subsequent analyses.

These methods and techniques are combined in different ways to drive the ways that business processes are adapted for customer centricity. Although these methods rely on different kinds of algorithms that are increasingly bundled within software tool suites, it is valuable to understand some aspects of how they work to support the determination of which kinds of analytical algorithms and models to use.

MARKET BASKET ANALYSIS

Market basket analysis is a process that looks for relationships among entities and objects that frequently appear together, such as the collection of items in a shopper's cart. For the purposes of customer

centricity, market basket analysis examines collections of items to identify affinities that are relevant within the different contexts of the customer touch points. Some examples include:

- Product placement—Identifying products that may often be purchased together and arranging the placement of those close by to
  encourage the purchaser to buy both items. That placement can be
  physical, such as in the arrangement of products on shelves in a
  brick and mortar location, or virtual, such as in a print catalog or
  on an e-commerce site.
- Point-of-Sale—Companies may use the affinity grouping of multiple
  products as an indication that customers may be predisposed to
  buying certain sets of products at the same time. This enables the
  presentation of items for cross-selling, or may suggest that customers may be willing to buy more items when certain products are
  bundled together.
- Customer retention—When customers contact a business to sever a
  relationship, a company representative may use market basket analysis to determine the right incentives to offer in order to retain the
  customer's business.

MEMORY-BASED REASONING

Memory-based reasoning (MBR) is a process of analyzing known historical situations to create predictive models in which new situations
are compared to find the closest matches that can then be reviewed to
inform choices. MBR can be used for classification, presuming that an
existing data set is used as the basis for determining classes (perhaps
by clustering) and then using the results to classify new objects. It can
also be used for prediction, via the same method as the matching process to find the closest match. The resulting behavior of that matching
context can be used to predict the outcome of the new scenario. This is
implemented in two steps:

1. Building the model using a training set of data and specific
   outcomes.
2. Using the model for comparison with new data instances.

The combination of customer classification and the MBR predictive
model provides suggestions for actions to take based on the customer's
class and the context of the specific scenario. This technique revolves

the concept of measuring similarity between pairs of objects, both during the training process and later, trying to match the new object to its closest neighbor within the classified set. This involves the use of a *similarity* (sometimes called *distance*) *function*, which measures how similar the members of any pair of objects are to each other, and a *combination function*, which is used to combine the results from the set of neighbors to arrive at a decision.

CLUSTER DETECTION

As we have already suggested, *clustering* is a key capability for any analytics toolbox intended to divide a given customer data set into smaller groups exhibiting some similarities. As with MBR, measuring similarities for clustering involves a distance function for comparison. Two approaches are used for clustering. In the first, there is an assumption or a directive regarding the number of clusters, and the objective is to divide the community into that number of clusters. The second approach attempts to grow the clusters organically—each customer starts out with his/her own cluster, and an iterative process attempts to merge clusters based on similarity of different attributes.

LINK ANALYSIS

Link analysis is a process of finding connections between different entities, such as connecting customers to other customers or customer to products. Link analysis not only establishes the connection, it also provides information about how other variables or attributes can be used to characterize the type of link as well as its strength. In particular, link analysis is critical for mapping and then understanding spheres of influence as discussed in Chapter 5, looking at various kinds of relationships and questions such as:

- Closely connected groups of customers.
- Collections of individuals linked by certain attributes such as location, purchased products, or other demographic variables.
- The speed at which communication flows across a social network.
- Which customers are known as having a particular expertise in using products.
- Which customers exercise significant influence over the broadest collection of individuals.

DECISION TREES

A *decision tree* is a decision-support model that encapsulates the questions and the possible answers and guides the analyst toward the appropriate result, and can be used for prediction models coupled with classification. Decision tree analysis looks at a collection of data instances and given outcomes, evaluates the frequency and distribution of values across the set of variables, and constructs a decision model in the form of a tree.

The nodes at each level of this tree represent a question, and each possible answer to the question is represented as a branch that points to another node at the next level. For example, we can have a binary decision tree where one internal node asks whether the customer's annual income is between $0 and $25,000, between $25,000 and $65,000, or greater than $65,000. If the answer is the first, the left-hand path is taken; if the second choice is selected, then the middle path is traversed; if the answer is the third, the right-hand path is taken. At each step along the path from the root of the tree to the leaves, the set of records that conform to the answers along the way continues to grow smaller.

Essentially, each node in the tree represents a way of subsetting the customer base in a way that conforms to the answers to the questions along the path one traverses to the specified node. Since each answer divides the set at that point by the number of possible answers, each node reflects a smaller community of individuals with a greater number of similarities among that subset. The predictive models can be integrated with the decision tree to drive specific actions at each customer touch point in reaction to the narrowed customer classes at each level of the tree.

MAKING ANALYTICS PART OF THE PROCESS

As shown in this chapter, there is a breadth of methods and algorithms for customer analytics. From the technical perspective, the challenges

Figure 9.3 Managing analytics feedback.

are twofold: figuring out what you are trying to learn and then figuring out which methods and algorithms to use. Partner with technologists and engage them as part of the customer centricity team. Integrating the technology team as part of the feedback loop (as we recall in Figure 9.3) will streamline the selection and use of best of breed tools and techniques for customer analytics.

CHAPTER 10

Making Customer Centricity Pervasive in the Company

INTRODUCTION

In spite of the considerable space dedicated to presenting approaches, techniques, and algorithms that can be used to enable a customer-centric strategy, awareness alone is insufficient to positively effect the desired outcomes. Executing the customer-centric strategy requires commitment from key stakeholders and skilled team members in the organization. It is critical that corporate leadership realizes the extent of the necessary coordination of people, processes, systems, and measurement techniques to take full advantage of customer analytics through integration across the spectrum of customer touch points. For a company to successfully enhance and create value results using these techniques, it requires a holistic deployment of customer-centric actions.

Systemic customer centricity demands corporate alignment and adjustments to organizational behavior to ensure a positive common customer experience. This implies the possibility of adjustments to the various interactions or other touch points throughout the various customer-facing business processes and scenarios, even when those changes may not be perceived to have immediate payoff!

For example, many organizations are so profit oriented and driven by their immediate expectations for profitability that they lose sight of the long-term benefits that can be achieved by treating their customers well even when it does not necessarily result in increased revenues. Yet deemphasizing or canceling customer-centric initiatives not only negatively impacts the company's ability to attract and acquire new customers, it also can lead to increased attrition of existing customers.

Because of the difficulty in tying an actual dollar value to customer-centric programs, the benefit gained by the company from these programs is sometimes not obvious. Often CFOs will look to cut these types of programs, not realizing that the customers they lose may represent a significant lifetime value.

Effectuating the benefits of a customer-centric program means that the organization needs to go through a corporate culture change so that the mindsets of staff members are aligned with the expectations of the program. Thought processes must be adjusted to ensure that the actions taken are always consistent with improving the customer experience. And probably most importantly, those changes need to begin at the top and trickle down throughout the organization. These changes must go beyond lip service and must be demonstrated in actions. This way, staff members can recognize senior-level commitment and credibility in changing the way the organization operates. In turn, integrating customer centricity across all aspects of the business will ease that transition.

TAKING IT FROM THE TOP

Customer centricity begins at the top. If employees are not presented with a consistent message from senior management, they cannot be expected to conform to the program expectations. The behavior and actions of senior management establish the level of credibility for the rest of the organization, and when the senior management's commitment is believed, the rest of the staff is more likely to follow their lead.

All levels of management need to identify actions that demonstrate that they actually support these types of customer-focused programs. Through management's actions, employees quickly assess what is important to their leadership and behave accordingly. Some examples of activities and actions that can be taken by senior staff, particularly those occupying the C-Level suites, include:

- Establishing regular meetings between senior leaders and key customers and communicating the results of those meetings with employees of the company.
- Promoting customer experience and customer satisfaction surveys.
- Reviewing the results of customer surveys with company staff to identify new opportunities for creating value.
- Establishing improvement plans based upon the survey results and suggesting regular measurements to assess improvements.

One thing should be clear: make organizational changes where necessary to ensure alignment among groups. Some organizations have created a Chief Customer Officer or a Customer Centricity Officer

(CCO) who is responsible for defining the company's customer strategy and is accountable for its execution. Those responsibilities typically include identifying policies, procedures, systems, and organizational changes that are necessary throughout the company to improve existing customer relationships as well as potential customer treatment related strategies for acquiring new customers. Responsibilities also include defining metrics and managing the organization to guarantee that the best effort is made to achieve the desired results.

OVERSEEING CHANGE MANAGEMENT

As can be surmised, instituting customer centricity involves oversight of the transitions in behavioral changes across the organization. One approach is to create a Customer Centricity Steering and Change Management Committee to manage and oversee these transitions. The CCO or another member of the senior management team might lead this committee. The committee should have representation from all affected operational groups within the company.

The committee would be responsible for identifying organizational and operational changes necessary for implementing customer centricity. This also includes coordinating the planning of those changes, then tracking and measuring the results. This process is somewhat iterative because as changes are introduced, issues may arise that need to be addressed by the committee, worked into the plan, and then communicated to the right groups within the company. This committee is ultimately responsible for identifying, planning, and managing the progression of the changes being made for the customer centricity initiative. Additionally, this committee should be communicating results throughout the organization and ensure that positive results are celebrated.

INCENTIVIZE GOOD BEHAVIOR THROUGH RECOGNITION AND REWARD

Employees will recognize the importance the company places on the customer-centric strategy by seeing how management rewards those who participate or take on leadership roles. The best way for an organization's leadership to help employees recognize the importance of these programs is by recognizing and rewarding those who embrace these initiatives and drive these initiatives to success. That will influence employees to look for ways to excel and stand out in the organization.

Individuals who have demonstrated measurable contributions to the customer-centric strategy can be recognized and rewarded in a number of ways, such as corporate-wide notice, monetary compensation, or even being selected for training for a special customer-oriented career path. These approaches help other members of the organization recognize behaviors and actions that are valued by the company's management.

ASSOCIATE EVERY JOB TO CUSTOMERS

One concern might be the fact that many staff members may be somewhat insulated from dealing directly with end users of the company's products and services. As you can imagine, when individuals are dissociated from dealing directly with the customers, it is very easy to see how they can lose touch with what's important from the customer's perspective. The challenge is communicating how typical operational activities have any kind of impact (positive or negative) on customer relationships.

As an example, consider the members of the corporate finance group who focus on the financial measures that roll up to the corporate bottom line. They often only look for ways to increase profitability by reducing company expenses. When they see initiatives that do not have clear and direct ties to immediate revenue generation, those initiatives are often viewed as consuming unnecessary expenses. Without any consideration of how an initiative that is currently being instituted may enable the company to enhance their ongoing and future relationships with existing or new customers, the finance team members may target the customer-centric projects to be cut.

In order to align an organization along the lines of customer centricity, every role and each set of tasks in the company must be tied to the potential positive or negative impacts on customer experience. New behaviors must be ingrained as part of the corporate culture.

To continue our example, train the members of the finance team to consider the potential impacts of their decisions and actions to the customer relationships. Even if some roles do not have clear ties to (or direct interactions) with the company's customers, it is necessary to cultivate those connections no matter who is involved in a business process. Making customer centricity a priority at the most senior levels of the organization will have a significant effect on influencing the behavior of staff members across the organization. Not only must the senior managers need to practice what they preach, they also need to make sure that every company role is provided some way to tie their actions to the customer's experience with the company.

REPLICATE BEST PRACTICES THROUGH MENTORSHIP PROGRAMS

There are employees who naturally understand the connections of their processes to the customers and will naturally embrace the cultural changes for customer centricity more quickly than others. Recognizing and rewarding these team players is one thing; engaging them to become trainers can help replicate their behavior among a larger cohort of employees.

One method is to document the positive customer-centric actions and approaches of these individuals and then include those best practices in a guide that can be shared throughout the organization. This can help permeate good practices through the organization. Making these individuals mentors to others is also often a positive way to encourage their behavior, provides them with appropriate recognition, and leverages their skills to help others begin to behave in a similar way to customer centricity more pervasive in the organization.

Internal mentorship programs can be jump-started using external experts to guide the transfer of knowledge. Seek those experts with experience deploying customer-centric strategies to help identify best practices for your organization and provide necessary training for members of your organization.

ALIGN OPERATIONAL AND ORGANIZATIONAL INTERFACES

Another challenge to enterprise-wide customer centricity is that organization by line of business isolates one area of the business from another. If the same community of customers purchases products and services from different divisions, there may be existing barriers that prevent visibility into a holistic view of the customer profile. When different parts of a company offer customers a variety of products and services while operating as multiple silos, additional effort must be expended to ensure that customers are treated consistently.

In other words, especially in siloed businesses, making the customer the center of attention requires a degree of cross-silo alignment of customer data acquisition, profiling, and assessment of the interdependency of interactions at different touch points. For example, a telecommunications company may engage the same customer for their home wireline telephone service, Internet, television, and wireless telephone service. In a siloed business, each of these lines of business may communicate with the same customer independently, even if the customer is unaware of the internal corporate division. As far as the customer is concerned, though, it is a nuisance to receive replicated calls, mailings, and emails all offering the same upsell or cross-sell opportunities.

In a customer-centric organization, the business owners would recognize the need to treat each unique customer as a single individual over the lifetime of the customer's relationship. This means on day one sending only one welcome letter no matter how many products or services were purchased or only sending one offer in the mail instead of three for the same product.

To accomplish the necessary integration, the leaders within each line of business must commit to sharing information and aligning business processes in relation to knowledge of customer profiles. This includes information integration, interoperable business processes, integrated systems, all engineered with a collaborative mindset.

It is often difficult to get the right level of cooperation across the different divisions to implement these changes. Senior leaders must demonstrate their agreement to the holistic, systemic nature of the customer-centric strategy to ensure that staff members within each division recognize the importance of their cooperation and support. This type of alignment cuts horizontally across organizations and operations and will necessarily contribute to achieving the anticipated benefits of customer centricity.

BE SELF-AWARE AND SELF-TRUTHFUL

Customer centricity is not a prerequisite to profitability; many organizations generate profits in the absence of any positive customer engagement. However, these are often businesses in which a captive audience is relegated to a limited choice of vendors, either because the market is a niche one, there is little competition, or the products are one-time-only purchases with no need to or advantage in developing an ongoing relationship with customers. In other cases, some products or services sufficiently satisfy the customer without significant follow-up engagement.

In these types of situations, there may not be a return on investment in implementing customer centricity initiatives. In any organization, there must be some key stakeholder group that can assess the value of a customer-centric strategy.

For example, it may be the marketing group within the company that will make the case to identify the value of customer centricity. If so, that group must take on the role of champion: develop the business case, convince the financial supporters to back the activity, and lay the groundwork for development of the program. Maintain consistency and provide ample time and support for customer-centric efforts to ensure that the initiatives will take hold and prove their value.

An inconsistent approach will send a mixed message to the employees, and worse, the customers. Consistency in leadership and engagement will promote credibility and lead to incremental adoption and eventual success. Identify small, more easily achievable customer centricity projects so that expectations can be more easily be managed across the organization, and iteratively increase their projects (and size of projects) as they lead to positive results.

NEXT STEPS: DEVELOPING THE PROGRAM PLAN

The evolution of customer centricity at an organization involves numerous smaller steps, as we have explored so far; these steps include:

- Define what customer centricity means within your organization.
- Identify the types of value that are critical to your company's mission and vision.
- Identify business expectations, define performance metrics, and link the customer experience to increased performance and value.

- Specify your different types of customers and clarify the different customer roles.
- Understand the customer interaction life cycle.
- Design your model for customer lifetime value.
- Map the relationships within the customer community.
- Isolate models of influence across the customer network.
- Enumerate the different customer interface scenarios.
- Identify the critical customer touch points and modes of interaction.
- Document the exchange of value at each customer interaction.
- Seek opportunities for increasing value in relation to each customer interaction.
- Determine the data entities and data elements necessary for developing a customer profile.
- Design, develop, and implement the models for customer profiling.
- Design, develop, and implement models for customer analysis.
- Implement the change management necessary to promote customer centricity across the enterprise.

However, any organization that is serious about committing to designing, developing, and deploying a strategy for customer centricity must allocate the right resources for scoping, planning, overseeing, and maintaining the program. The foundation for this program plan must be laid prior to any accumulation of data, acquisition of tools, or development of analytical models. Unless the plan is in place to ensure that the right steps are to be taken, there are server limitations to the creation of value.